Fun Inc.

Tom Chatfield is one of the UK's most prominent young commentators on digital culture. A speaker at forums including TED Global, authors@Google, the House of Commons, the RSA, the World Congress on IT, and the Labour and Conservative party conferences, he's also a contributor to publications including the *Observer*, *Sunday Times*, *Independent*, *Wired*, *New Statesman* and *TLS*, and a senior editor and lead writer at *Prospect* magazine.

Tom completed a doctorate at St John's College, Oxford, before moving to London to work as a full-time writer and editor. He has done puzzle design and creative consultancy for a number of online games and media companies, including Mind Candy, Grex, Red Glasses and Intervox, and is currently working on a project with award-winning British games company Preloaded. He speaks regularly on technology and digital culture in the national and international media.

Fun Inc.

Why games are the twenty-first
century's most serious business

Tom Chatfield

First published in 2010 by Virgin Books, an imprint of Ebury Publishing
A Random House Group Company

This updated edition first published in 2011 by Virgin Books

2 4 6 8 10 9 7 5 3 1

The Random House Group Limited Reg. No. 954009

Addresses for companies within the Random House Group can be
found at www.randomhouse.co.uk

A CIP catalogue record for this book is available
from the British Library

The Random House Group Limited supports The Forest Stewardship
Council [FSC], the leading international forest certification organisation.
All our titles that are printed on Greenpeace-approved FSC-certified
paper carry the FSC logo. Our paper procurement policy can be found
at www.rbooks.co.uk/environment

Mixed Sources
Product group from well-managed
forests and other controlled sources
www.fsc.org Cert no. TT-COC-2139
© 1996 Forest Stewardship Council

Typeset in Sabon by Palimpsest Book Production Limited,
Falkirk, Stirlingshire

Printed and bound in Great Britain by
CPI Bookmarque Ltd, Croydon CR0 4TD

ISBN: 978 0 7535 19455

For Mum, Dad and my wife, Cat

Contents

	Preface	ix
1	The fun instinct	1
2	Technology and magic	13
3	A license to print money	27
4	A beautiful science	39
5	Dangerous playground	55
6	The Warcraft effect	87
7	Clouds and flowers	111
8	Second lives	135
9	Serious play	153
10	Beyond fun	181
11	Future Inc.?	209
	Epilogue	229
	Bibliography and ludography	235
	Acknowledgements	243
	Index	247

Preface

In April 2008, my friend Jon flew from North Carolina to visit me in England. Jon manages a store in a small town in Gaston County, just outside Charlotte, and this was the first time he'd travelled outside America; he'd had to get his first ever passport for the trip. It was also the first time we'd met face to face, although we'd known each other for almost two years.

Jon and I met in *World of Warcraft*, a game that my wife and I have played ever since it launched in 2004. The three of us started out helping each other with in-game tasks. Then, as we got to know each other better, we moved on to talking through microphones and headsets while playing. We swapped emails, linked up on Facebook, discussed books and films, and pieced together the details of our very different lives. Jon was smart, in his early twenties and had dropped out of college due to funding difficulties; my wife and I were working long hours in medicine and publishing, and *World of Warcraft* offered us a sociable, absorbing evening "out," away from the pressures of daily life.

We often think of video games – and of digital culture in

general – as a substitute for worldly encounters, and a troubling one at that. Yet our appetite for the digital has grown hand in hand with an increasing recognition of the value of the live and the interpersonal; and, above all, of the importance of the social aspects of technology. More than anything else, it is these sociable, interpersonal forces that are driving forward the next stages of the digital revolution. Jon was the first gaming friend of mine to visit us in London, but not the last: since his stay, several others have made the journey across the Atlantic, while my wife and I have travelled up and down America's east coast visiting and staying with people we first got to know through video games.

This book was first published in January 2010, and largely written and researched during 2009. As I write these words, in October 2010, video games are still less than half a century old. Over the two years since I began writing this book, around a hundred million new people have begun to explore this youngest and most dynamic of our media; and yet decades of evolution and expansion remain ahead.

The great momentum of the current movement in games comes thanks not to the triumphs of big-budget blockbusters (although these have played their part) but to the interconnected explosion of casual, mobile and sociable games. Wherever technology takes us, one of our most fundamental impulses is to play; and in the form of smart mobile devices, linked via social networks, technology is rapidly taking us all into a place this book is dedicated to exploring: a world where the boundaries between work, leisure, play, profit and personal relations are ever more blurred.

This is a shamelessly partisan book about video games, and

I make no apologies for that. Alongside my work over the last decade teaching literature, working as an arts and books editor, and speaking and writing about the frontiers of digital culture, my experience of games has been a hugely enriching part of my life. This is something I hope to share and explore. And I believe it is something the world is increasingly ready to embrace.

Across all media, from literature to music to film, the visual and intellectual language of gaming is gaining ground as an integral part of global culture. The lessons games can teach – from engagement and reward structures to visualisation technologies, motion-responsive interfaces and sociological analytics – are beginning to be taken seriously across business, education, government and art alike.

Controversies have always proliferated around the world of video games, and seem likely to continue to do so, about violence and censorship; but also about the more nebulous fields of addiction, security, transparency, intellectual property and personal identity. This book, I hope, offers a firm grounding in the debates surrounding these, and a guide to where the genuine controversies lie in a field plagued with hysteria, ignorance and unjustifiable generalisations alongside justifiable fears.

This isn't, however, a book about why games are 'good' any more than it can be a repudiation of why they are not 'bad.' As anyone who loves games will concede, 90 per cent of the titles out there are simply not good enough. In everything from their artistic merit to their playability, design and execution, they could be better. Sometimes they are awful, objectionable, banal, or simply not enjoyable. This is to be expected. Contrary to the popular myth of electronic entertainments as implacable engines of manipulation, it is very difficult indeed to make a decent video game, let alone an excellent one. It does no damage to literature or to cinema to say that most books and films are flawed, limited, or trivial. The same is true of games. This is the nature of any medium, and of excellence.

Wanting video games to be better is a central part of loving them. But the anatomy and criticism of games is a task for a different book to this one. Indeed, it's a task already being undertaken with considerable sophistication and relish both online and in print. What I hope to achieve is something simpler and more fundamental: to explore why video games are worth taking seriously in the first place; to suggest the nature and range of the discussions it is worth having around them; and to show how these discussions may help us to understand our culture's increasing augmentation and amplification by technology.

If there is an underlying message here, it is of continuity, not transformation. To face the future hopefully, together with its technology, we must remember that humans themselves are much the same as we ever were. It is only our possibilities of being and action that have changed: we are more stimulated, more distracted, more interconnected, more challenged, more able to learn, more able to lose ourselves than ever before.

In a field defined by constant innovation, the contents of this book are already some distance from the cutting edge. Appropriately enough for a book about games, almost every number you read about will, in the last twelve months, have gone up. I'm not too worried about this. By far the most interesting things about both video games and people are those that will not transform in the space of twelve months, twelve years, or even half a century. The reasons that games exert so deep and broad an appeal are ancient, and if we're to have any hope of understanding the future more than a year at a time, we must take the long perspective.

Looking at the transformations the coming decade is certain to bring, one word in particular seems in urgent need of retirement: "gamers," that segment of the population who know and play video games. For there is fast becoming no "us" or "them" when it comes to games. In 2009, the National Gamers Survey reported that 83% of the US population played video games, including 72% of men and women over 50. In the UK, the figure was 73%, including over 90% of those under twenty. Whatever your opinion on video games, they will soon be universal. Within another generation they will have their place in every home and every pocket, as inevitable as a computer or mobile phone. This is neither a dreadful nor a marvellous fact: it is simply an aspect of the world we must learn to live with and understand as best we can.

We need to take this word "gamers" and throw it away, together with all those other generalizations that open up no debate and that mask the future under vague hopes and wild fears. For we need to talk seriously about the world as it is: about how to get the best out of its media, where the worst really lies, and what the games we play can tell us about ourselves and our future. The news is assuredly not all good. But we cannot afford not to listen.

CHAPTER 1

The Fun Instinct

I was born in 1980, in England, just outside London. And this meant that my childhood was full of something that simply didn't exist for anyone born just a couple of decades before me: video games.

My first gaming experience came when I was seven, in the form of a BBC Micro Model B. Affectionately known as a 'Beeb', and manufactured by Acorn Computers between 1981 and 1986, it looked like the lovechild of a toaster and an obese typewriter: a weightily off-white chunk of plastic that beeped alarmingly and shouted 'Mistake' at you in bald bright type if you dared approach it unprepared. It could display just eight colours on its minuscule monitor, while its 32-kilobyte memory would be put to shame by most modern watches. Yet this machine – in combination with the 400 closely typed pages of its ring-bound manual – was my one-way ticket to the information age.

There were plenty of primitive graphical games to be played on the Beeb but, as I soon discovered, it was quite a different kind of play that was first to captivate me: games which consisted entirely of words. Sometimes called 'adventure' games, you had to make your way around a host of fictional universes by typing compass directions and basic instructions ('pick up the torch', 'look at the elvish sword') and by reading a series of second-person descriptions ('you are in a maze of twisty little passages, all alike'). Today, it all sounds impossibly crude. Yet once I began to play my way through a text adventure, I found within minutes that the machine's technological limitations had melted away, and in their place came the dizzy excitement of walking into a story. As the pioneering text games company Infocom puts it, its products had 'the best graphics in the world'. Why draw a travesty of a castle in blocky pixels when it was possible to describe the most glorious building imaginable in a couple of sentences? Video games, I began to realise, were much more than mere toys: they were a way of exploring, and attempting to create, whole other worlds.

Video games also represented my first taste of a modernity that definitively excluded adults: a realm of private codes, toy universes and bleeping music that seemed several thousand miles away from books, television and school. To play the best games was to be transported dizzyingly away from the mundane to become the hero of a favourite adventure or an explorer on another planet. But it was also to engage with technology, logic, narrative, design and creative collaboration. My friends and I spent many hours designing and critiquing games, anxious to achieve the perfect balance, the most thrilling narrative, the most cunning puzzle.

In many ways, the miraculously intense and sustained kind of fun that video games offered relied on the absence of actual consequences or responsibilities. They were, as our parents would occasionally note, childish, not just in their subject-matter, but in their ecstatic unreality. Yet there was also something about even these early games that felt far more significant and more serious than anything else we had ever called a 'game': a sense similar to the vertigo that the best books and stories could inspire, of finding the world spun around in new and unexpected ways.

Looking back, it's clear that video games were not just a portal to other worlds: they were also a window through which we were glimpsing a part of the world's future. Today, three decades on, the upper limits of virtual worlds continue to retreat before our eyes. Companies can now create online games that can be accessed by many millions of players and that require hundreds of artists and technicians to collaborate in their creation, and still we have only begun to scratch the surface of what can be achieved. My generation has grown into adulthood, yet we have not set aside our computers and our consoles; instead, we have brought them with us.

It was words that first drew me to video games, and words that first gave me a taste of their power. While it might seem incongruous to have written a book about an electronic medium, the kind of sustained analysis that the written word offers is still the most important tool we have for making sense of our own experience. Media can compete for our time and attention while remaining mutually enriching; far from being at opposite poles, I believe books and games are both compatible and complementary, being the two great 'active' media of our time. It's not for nothing that the internet is, among other things, a supreme arena of exchange for the written word in all its forms.

This book is about the astonishing leaps that the last few decades have seen in the automation, incorporation, refinement and extension of the deep human sense that – for want of a better word – we call fun. Games have a history as old as civilisation itself; computers and the internet have existed for barely the blink of an eye. And yet the latter has been colonised and shaped so thoroughly by the former that it's becoming increasingly hard to tell where the serious business of play ends and the playful business of work begins.

Video games are just one subset of the grand category of games: structured activities carried out for pleasure, according to certain written or unwritten rules. Games are as old as civilisation itself and are found in all cultures. Evidence survives of competitive game-playing from as early as 2600 BC, while archaeologists have found game 'boards' that were apparently scratched onto the backs of statues by bored Assyrian guards in the eighth century BC. Humans have been playing games for at least as long as we have been reading, writing and perhaps even speaking – and this latest great resurgence of gameplaying has deep roots in both our cultural and our biological history.

The urge to play is universal, not just in human cultures but among higher animals. From ants to birds to monkeys, playful rituals such as mock-fighting allow animals to test, improve and even celebrate their being in the world. It is only humans, however, that play games in the strict sense. A play-fight between primates may obey the most elaborate kind of unwritten rules, but only humans are able to codify their games independently of themselves. We are rule-making (and rule-seeking) creatures, and our love of order extends to play.

The modern world's attitude towards games is itself an odd mixture of the dismissive and the deeply committed. In the case of sports, at no point in history has any activity commanded as much attention as sporting endeavour. The 2010 football World Cup was, thanks to the reach of modern media, was watched at some point by over three billion people. At the time of writing, this was the single greatest collective experience in human history. Similarly, for all its compromises, the modern Olympics is perhaps the greatest human festival of internationalism in history.

And yet games are rigidly separated in the minds of most people from the serious business of work and living. The entire industry of contemporary leisure thrives on this separation between work and play. You work, and you spend a significant proportion of your income on leisure, but the two are mutually exclusive; each invokes its own rigid, and seemingly incompatible set of conventions. Work entails a degree of self-sacrifice, dedication, effort and, hopefully, the satisfaction that comes from earning your keep. Games, meanwhile, are about escaping into a mindset where pleasure rules: the whole point is that there is nothing resting on the outcome of the game beyond the value you personally choose to attach to it.

Work, then, seems to be about rules, restrictions and necessities, whereas a game is about pleasure, freedom and escape from urgent need. Nevertheless, all games can also be thought of as little more than an exceptionally rigid set of rules and ideas. Consider the popular board game, Pictionary, in which players compete to draw recognisable versions of as many objects as they can for other people to guess. Within the box of a Pictionary set you'll find a board, playing pieces, a die, a timer, some paper, some cards with lists of items on, and some pencils. Apart from the board and the cards – which are just a way of measuring progress and providing a list of things to draw – these are everyday items. By packing them up in a box with a set of instructions, however, they are transformed into nothing less than a formal declaration of the desire to play. The purchase of these objects is a kind of licence, buying a space and a time outside the ordinary run of things within which the avowed intent is pleasure.

During a game of Pictionary, the players' main activity is drawing on scraps of paper. It's something they could have done pretty much any time, had they had the inclination. What is it, then, that makes the game? In one sense, the game is born of a consensus: the learning and obeying of a simple set of rules. This consensus allows both competition and collaboration; it allows the measurement of better and worse performances, of more and less achievement. It allows players the satisfaction of showing off their skills, and of achieving something measurable. Since 2001 there has even been such a thing as the World Championship of Pictionary: create a challenge, and there will always be people whose greatest pleasure is demonstrably being the best. Create a game at which there is little or no skill, or opportunity for distinction, and the result will soon be boredom.

Yet part of the charm of a game like Pictionary is that it is about more than simply crushing your opponents. The drawing component of the game is at least as much about self-expression and incidental delight as it is about competing – an excuse for a controlled few moments of disinhibition. To play it is as much to be creative and sociable as it is to compare skills and achievements. It is a team game, whose greatest satisfactions involve successful communication and interactions above and beyond the raw mechanics of the game itself.

The end product is a complex and powerful set of human motivators: achievement, competition, collaboration, learning and improvement, communication and self-expression. And what makes them a 'game', as opposed to something more serious, is the avowedly non-functional context they are framed in – the box, the label, the time set aside for pleasure rather than labour.

Of course, playing a video game doesn't require consensus or rule-learning in the way that something like football, chess or Pictionary does. You're not strolling on to a patch of grass holding a ball or unpacking a box full of pencils and paper. You are, rather, being presented with a miniature but complete world whose rules are an integral part of its structure – something that has been elaborately crafted down to its tiniest detail. If it's well designed, you can no more disobey those rules than you can cheat at football by floating across the pitch in defiance of gravity.

With a football or a pack of cards, there are hundreds of games you can theoretically play. In a video game, you can only do what the game allows you to. The world of the game itself embodies its rules, and your job is to puzzle them out. Like the real world, video games are arenas into which you're dropped and left to deduce a method of success for yourself. You can progress only by gaining experience; and the skills that this experience taps into are some of the most fundamental human motivations there are.

Within the increasingly distinguished field of video games studies, perhaps the most influential person to have discussed these fundamental motivations is the designer and author Raph Koster. Koster has, among other things, worked as lead designer on *Ultima Online* (1997), the world's first commercially successful massively multiplayer online game (MMO), and as creative director on another MMO milestone, *Star Wars Galaxies* (2003), based on the *Star Wars* universe. He's also the author of an influential book, *A Theory of Fun for Game Design* (2004), that was one of the first to set out in precise terms the special relationship between people's minds and the games they play:

Games are something special and unique. They are concentrated chunks ready for our brains to chew on. Since they are abstracted and iconic, they are readily absorbed. Since they are formal systems, they exclude distracting external details. Usually, our brains have to do hard work to turn messy reality into something as clear as a game is.

Learning, Koster explains, is something humans find extraordinarily satisfying, because the ability to learn certain kinds of lessons is perhaps our most vital trait in evolutionary terms. Uniquely, we have become able to learn as both individuals and as a species; we learn as individuals, but we also pass on our knowledge from generation to generation.

In the thousands upon thousands of years during which modern man has evolved, the desire and ability to learn – and the aptitude for solving all manner of spatial, hierarchical, conceptual and relational problems – has ensured both our survival and, over time, our dominance of the earth. It should come as little surprise, then, that the mastery of certain kinds of learning challenge thrills us like little else.

Seen in these terms, video games emerge as an extraordinary kind of reverse-engineering. Our brains were moulded over hundreds of thousands of years by the necessity of surviving in the world. And yet, today, the brains that we developed as a result of this are now busily creating other unreal worlds designed expressly to satisfy them.

The word 'fun', here, can itself be misleading. Why use a word with such a ring of simplicity, even of childishness, in such a complex context? 'It's the word we are stuck with,' Koster responds when I put this question to him. 'There isn't even consensus across the European languages as to what exactly to call this vague, general feeling that in English is called fun. As a concept, it varies radically from language to language.' And yet – like humour, another vital area of human sentiment whose very nature defies analysis – we are all able to recognise fun when we experience it. It is a slippery, vital notion that speaks of something mysterious in all of us: the desire to draw not only physical and immediate gratifications from the world, but to make a game of our being.

What of video games in particular? 'First,' Koster notes, 'you have to look at games in general, and how they differ from other media. What games do that no other medium does is provide experiential learning, which is fundamentally an iterative experience; you do it again and again, learning a bit more each time. What video games do very differently from, say, board games is that they provide a model with a very rapid simulation.' And that means what, exactly? 'When you poke and prod at them, you can get feedback extremely quickly, and often at a fundamental visceral level. Or, their model can be slow to respond but be extremely complex – far more complex than what you could manage with counters on a board.'

Of course, 'visceral' thrills are often thought of as the most fundamental components of our pleasure-seeking: speed, jaw-dropping sounds and images, thudding violence, adrenaline-pumping action, sex. Modern video games are certainly able to offer these in abundance. They grab our attention, they make headlines, they offer short-term gratification. And yet the visceral is ultimately beside the point. Even in the most stunning-looking, ultra-violent video game imaginable, there will rapidly come a point at which players realise that what makes the experience of playing meaningful is something more symbolic than literal. Even the most intense initial excitement will soon give way to boredom unless there is something else there that is, in Koster's term, sufficiently 'chewy'.

As an example of the 'something else' that can lift a video game beyond mere novelty into the realm of serious fun, Koster cites 'a game called *M.U.L.E.* by Dani Bunten Berry as my favourite game of all time. It is a classic multiplayer video game of planetary colonization and economics, played on eight-bit computers in the early 1980s. I love it so much I have it running on my phone.' *M.U.L.E.* is also a game that lacks anything even remotely resembling a visceral thrill. Originally written for the Atari 400 home computer in 1983, it's a turn-based strategy game for up to four players in which each side must manage a space colony, balancing the harvesting of energy, food, metal ore and valuable minerals with the buying and selling of these resources to each other or to a central 'store'.

Visually, it's considerably less sophisticated than the display on a modern mobile phone. The game's title refers to the machines that players must build and use in their harvesting activities, Multiple Use Labor Elements (that is, M.U.L.E.s). And that, apart from periodic random indignities such as assault by space pirates, is that. Except, as Koster notes, beneath the simple rules lies something entrancingly complex. 'The thing that makes this game so fascinating to play to this day is the amazingly simple way in which it creates so many emergent behaviours. It is a game where competition and cooperation exist on a razor's edge. You want to be the most successful colonist, but if you are too cut-throat then the colony as a whole will fail. You have to specialize to get ahead, but that makes you dependent on the other players for survival.'

This notion of 'emergent behaviours' is a central one in video game theory. Essentially, it describes what happens when a complex system arises out of a simple set of interactions. It's a concept common in science and philosophy: the universe itself can be thought of as the miraculously complex product of small a number of basic rules. Similarly, in the miniature universes of the best video games, it's the ability of simple, well-worked rules with to yield an exponentially emerging complexity that most seems to tick our evolutionary boxes.

From the simplest of parameters, then, video games conjure engagements that echo the evolving, multi-factorial complexities humanity has been engaging with for millennia. And yet, as the next chapter explores, their own brief history itself represents an evolution of incredible rapidity and scope.

CHAPTER 2

Technology and magic

'Any sufficiently advanced technology is indistinguishable from magic' wrote the science fiction novelist Arthur C Clarke in 1973, giving the computer age one of its most memorable maxims. Had Clarke, who died in 2008, lived just a year longer, he would have been able to see a piece of technology being demonstrated at a 2009 Expo in Los Angeles that looked, to many in the audience, very close to magic indeed.

The machine, perched on a black conical stand, looked like nothing so much as an oversized television remote control. It was a tracking box, and it combined the functions of a video camera, depth sensor, multi-array microphone and custom processor – meaning that it was able to follow the movements of up to four people standing in front of it while also recognising each individual's face and voice. It did this by constructing a visual map of each person, based on forty-eight points identified on their bodies according to shape and skeletal structure. This also meant that it could, as was demonstrated, continue to follow people's movements and differentiate between them even when they walked in front of one another. 'Use your own gear,' a demonstration video boasted, showing a woman using the sensor to try out clothes onscreen on a virtual reproduction of her body, followed by a boy holding up his skateboard so that its appearance could be scanned in and reproduced on a virtual counterpart.

The tracking box is known today as 'Kinect', and it represents some of the most sophisticated hardware and software ever created in the field of motion capture and wireless control. Kinect is also a device built primarily for play. Specifically, it is an add-on for Microsoft's Xbox 360 games console, and is due to be released in November 2010 into the mass market. The Kinect project, Steven Spielberg declared after the Los Angeles demonstration, represents 'a wave of change, the ripples of which will reach far beyond video games'. He was probably right: the potential of such a system for transforming the way people interact with technology within their own homes is immense. Already, there's talk of social networking involving full-body projections, of *Minority Report*-style virtual screens, of integration with true three-dimensional displays, virtual reality applications and much else besides. The device itself is likely to retail at a little over £100, offering an affordability that's almost as startling as its capabilities.

While it may mean a wave of change for the world at large, the kind of advance that the Kinect project represents has long been the exception rather than the rule for the video games industry. Since its birth, video gaming has been a business devoted to miracles. As Arthur C Clarke also wrote, 'The only way of finding the limits of the possible is by going beyond them into the impossible.' Video games represent a perpetual pressure on these limits: since the very beginning, they have been one of the most astounding engines the world possesses for creative and technological change.

In 1961, the Massachusetts Institute of Technology purchased one of the most advanced computing machines on the planet, a PDP-1 (Programmed Data Processor). MIT's model cost over $100,000 and was the size of a small telephone booth – impressively compact by the standards of the day. At a time when the world contained only a few thousand computers, most of which still filled entire rooms, this unit with a primitive keyboard and monitor display was about as personal as computing got.

The PDP-1 was, like every early computer, dauntingly difficult to approach. Programming it was a task intended to be undertaken only by experts working in the higher realms of logic and computational maths. It was the province of an intellectual elite, and it remained so right up to the point at which a small group of science fiction-obsessed students decided that there had to be more that a machine this powerful could do than simply crunch patterns of numbers. There had to be, they reasoned, a way of showing anyone who cared to find out just how great its potential truly was.

The leader of this group was Stephen 'Slug' Russell and, as he later described it, they formulated three criteria for an 'ultimate' program: something that would reveal the true potential of the machine sitting in their university. The program should 'demonstrate as many of the computer's resources as possible, and tax those resources to the limit'. It should 'be interesting, which means every run should be different'. And, most important of all, 'It should involve the onlooker in a pleasurable and active way.'

The future of computing, they had intuited, lay not just in the calculational prowess of ever more powerful machines, but in the far more uncertain field of human-machine interactions. Russell and his friends had worked out, in other words, that just about the most interesting and impressive thing it was possible to do with a computer was to create a game within it.

One year and 200 hours of programming later, the world's first true computer game was born. There had been primitive demonstration 'games' on earlier machines before, but this was the first time that any genuinely interactive play had been achieved; and it went by the name of *Spacewar!* In accordance with Russell's design criteria, its aim could be grasped within moments, although the actual mechanics were tricky to master. The PDP-1's monitor represented space, lightly dusted with stars (one MIT student later programmed in a real star map to make the effect as convincing as possible). Against this background, two human players entered into combat, each controlling their own spaceship – one shaped like a needle, the other like a wedge. At the centre of the screen pulsed a deadly star whose gravity constantly attempted to suck the players in. They could assault each other by firing tiny missiles out of the front of their ships, while limited fuel supplies gave the proceedings an element of urgency and a scoring system kept track of victories. Fifteen years before *Star Wars*, computerised space combat had come to the world's screens.

Spacewar! was the first miracle in gaming: it took one of the most complex machines ever created and instantly showed any user exactly why computing was so powerful a field. Here was a portal to a new destination in human experience, a space where people could interact in real time within an entirely simulated environment – as if a work of fiction had suddenly become real. Here, too, was one of the very first examples of a graphical interface on a computer. Long before the invention of the mouse, when ticker tape was still the standard input method for computers, *Spacewar!* offered its users interactive objects that they could freely move around a screen. It required no expert knowledge or training. This was computing as it had never been seen before: intuitive, exciting, universal.

At least as significant as its technical achievement was *Spacewar!*'s effect on other computer users. The program was so effective a use of the PDP-1's abilities that the computer's manufacturers began incorporating a version of *Spacewar!* as standard in the core memory of new models in order to test them. The game proved not only an effective test, but also a tutor of the most inspirational kind for students, staff and visitors alike. As MIT faculty member Albert W Kufeld, writing in July 1971, recalled, 'The first few years of *Spacewar!* at MIT were the best. The game was in a rough state, students were working their hearts out improving it, and the faculty was nodding benignly as they watched. The students were learning computer theory faster and more painlessly than they'd ever done before.' Around the world, clones, modifications and expansions of *Spacewar!* began to crop up in what could be described as the first viral spread of a computing meme. Students who had never shown any interest in mathematics were being drawn in, competing to push newer machines still further and to build a better game. The abstract had become enthrallingly human.

It was only a matter of time before people began to realise that *Spacewar!* represented not only a demonstration of computer technology's power, but also an unprecedented opportunity to make money. And perhaps the most significant of these people was another MIT student, Nolan Bushnell, who in 1971 collaborated with programmer Ted Dabney on an innovation that would finally transfer electronic gaming from hugely expensive institutional computers into the realm of the general public. Along the way, too, they would give many people their very first taste of computing as an affordable and even an accessible technology.

Bushnell and Dabney realised that, although building a programmable mainframe computer was well beyond any domestic budget, it was possible to construct a single-purpose circuit board into which the mechanics of a game were hardwired. This could then be mass-produced for relatively little money, and consumers charged to take turns in playing. Their first collaboration, based on *Spacewar!*, was a poorly designed flop. But they regrouped, founded a new company by the name of Atari, and released their second title: a ping-pong simulator involving two white bats, one at each side of the screen, bouncing a ball between them. It was called *Pong*, and it appeared at the end of 1972 in the form of a hulking wooden cabinet equipped with a screen, two primitive control 'paddles' and a slot for users to push coins through. The arcade machine had arrived.

Pong was neither the first commercial video game nor even an original idea. In fact it was based on an almost identical game that had appeared earlier that year on the world's first home gaming machine, the Magnavox Odyssey (whose inventor, Ralph Baer, is remembered today as the inventor of the first commercial video game, and the originator of the key insight that a television set hooked up to the right machine could be used for more than merely watching television programmes). In a sign of things to come, however, poor marketing decisions meant that the Magnavox Odyssey struggled to make an impression on public consciousness, and it was Atari's arcade version of *Pong* that claimed the title of the world's first video gaming hit.

'Avoid missing ball for high score' was the sole instruction *Pong* offered. Actuality had been boiled down to its simplest imaginable form – into an almost Platonic exercise in reaction times and spatial reasoning. Nevertheless it was enough and, virtually single-handedly, *Pong* transformed the world's relationship with computing technology. Here was something advanced and yet absolutely accessible. If a computer could be taught to do this, what else might it be able to conjure? By 1973, demand was such that *Pong* machines were being

19

shipped internationally – and imitated endlessly. An industry had been born.

Over the next decade, successors to *Pong* in the arcades and the Magnavox Odyssey in homes would sell tens of millions of copies, with games like *Space Invaders* (1978) and *Pac-Man* (1980) becoming the first icons of the gaming world. Long before the personal computer was a household fixture, an entire generation had been given a glimpse of the future – where there was an interactive screen in every household, and the most triumphant business strategy of all would be to get consumers playing.

Today, a video game can be either a casual or a deeply immersive business; a free slice of online fun, or a thousand-hour epic of intense skill and concentration. In each case, though, it remains locked to the promise of those early days – that, within a programmable machine, it is possible to create a uniquely engaged, compelling kind of interactive experience.

Having been born in a technology institute, gaming began its commercial life in a related but rather junior social niche, as a pursuit for teenage males. Both radio and television had started out in the living room, listened to and watched by families. The rise of mass print media was driven by public education and the universal demand for information; the cinema was from the beginning a mass entertainment for all ages; the possibilities for sound recording were self-evident even in its first decade. Video games, however, arrived looking at first glance like nothing so much as an extremely clever toy. And the story of their development and nature is one of incremental progress towards wider recognition, and of the gradual realisation of a promise that – for those who knew where to look – was there from the very beginning.

Over the course of the 1970s, Atari grew into a dominant force both at home and in the arcades. In the early 1980s, however, a number of commercial missteps and the low quality of many new games left the market in crisis, with critics claiming that video gaming had been little more than a passing fad. The industry, it seemed, was collapsing under the weight of its own amateurism. Yet it was at this point that gaming crossed one of its early watersheds, with the arrival of two Japanese companies – Nintendo and Sega – into what was about to become a truly international market place.

The Japanese firms were different from everything that had come before. They brought with them a new level of specialisation and quality, coupled to the principle of strictly controlling who was and wasn't allowed to develop products for their home gaming machines (known, increasingly, as consoles). It was a recipe for growing professionalism, production values and profits, as well as for a technological arms race that would see the graphical and processing capacities of consoles pushed forward at an increasingly startling rate.

A decade after they first began to distribute outside of Japan, Nintendo and Sega were the acknowledged kings of the gaming world and the most bitter of commercial rivals. This was the age of 'console wars'. Between 1985 and 1995, they sold between them over 100 million hardware units, and many hundreds of millions of games. The principle of games as electronic toys was, it seemed, approaching a high-water mark, with Nintendo increasingly the dominant player and Sega starting to overreach in its efforts to keep up. This particular brand of fun had saturated the teen and pre-teen market: where was it to go next?

As it turned out, the games industry had only just begun to transform itself. And the next stage of its evolution came courtesy of a newcomer to the industry, electronics giant Sony. Following a failed collaboration with Nintendo on a new console, Sony decided to go it alone and in 1995 released a games machine called the PlayStation. Other rivals to Sega and Nintendo had come and gone, including a belated and ill-advised attempt to re-enter the games console market from Atari. But the Sony PlayStation was different. Sleek, grey, expensively marketed and blisteringly powerful, it offered CD-quality sounds and gorgeous graphics at a heavily subsidized low price. It was something more than a must-have toy for teenagers: a desirable consumer product for young, upwardly mobile adults, complete with soundtracks designed for its launch titles by some of the hottest DJs on the global club scene.

The PlayStation was a bet on the claim that Stephen Russell had made three decades previously – that games were for everyone, and that their natural place was at the forefront of society's relationship with technology. Astonishingly to most observers, Sony's gamble was rewarded by its transformation into the world's most influential games company, with the PlayStation going on to sell 102 million units during its lifetime, and its successor enjoying still greater success. The market for video games was, the world realised, far broader and deeper than most people had ever believed.

Sony's ascendancy proved a knockout blow for Sega, which stopped making new consoles after 1998. Yet gaming was far from done with transformations, and the dramatic next stage of its evolution came thanks to Nintendo and their release, in 2006, of another entirely new kind of games console: the Wii (a name chosen, according to Nintendo, because 'Wii sounds like "we", which emphasises that the console is for everyone'). Ending once and for all the increasingly ruinous race for more potent technology, the Wii was a less expensive, less powerful alternative to the other machines on the market. But it had one great innovation – motion-sensitive controllers – coupled to a philosophy that chimed exactly with the sentiments of a new generation of gamers: that modern games could be not only a mainstream activity, but also something family-friendly, physically active, sociable and, above all, fun. It made a phenomenal impression, outselling its competitors by a factor of almost two to one, and left the video games market looking more wide open than ever.

Behind all of this, the slow, steady rise of the personal computer has continued: a story of gradually accumulating resources rather than the generational revolutions of games consoles, and one that leaped to a whole new level with the invention of the internet. Computers, unlike consoles, are an open platform. The divide between Macs and PCs notwithstanding, almost any computer can run at least one version of almost any game or program, something that has in the past restricted companies' opportunities for maximising their gaming profits on computers. But the unrestricted freedom to browse the internet that computers offer (unlike consoles, which give online access only to the 'walled gardens' that their manufacturers are able exclusively to control) means that literally millions of games are now at the fingertips of their users. And with game-playing now a more popular online activity than anything else outside of search and social networking, the evidence for play as one of the most fundamental social and economic dynamics of the present century – and the internet as its natural home – is mounting.

In terms of human hours, the internet is already the world's most important gaming arena, and it is also here that gaming's potential and its underlying nature can be seen with the greatest clarity. It is a phenomenon that brings people together while simultaneously allowing them to escape the world, either for a few minutes of casual fun, or for an entire other realm of adventures, achievements and shared experiences. There is remarkable potential and peril in this, on a scale that can begin to seem almost anti-human in its superlatives: the size, the scope, the sheer hours of effort consumed by electronic play in return for what can seem, to outsiders' eyes, scant rewards. But just as games have a particular history that has brought them to this point, they also remain not an implacable natural phenomenon, but the products of a human industry with its particular traits and foibles. This is an industry that has grown astonishingly fast – but that has not yet, in some ways, quite grown up. And in this the games industry echoes the attitude of many of its consumers, who are aware they are standing on the edge of something transforming; but not yet aware of just how much it may change them.

CHAPTER 3

A license to print money

At a time when most global media are either shrinking or static, perhaps the most noteworthy fact about the video games industry is its growth. At the end of the 1970s, global gaming was worth a few billion dollars a year. By the 1990s, software sales – that is, sales of the games themselves, rather than the machines they were played on – had moved past the $10 billion mark. Soon after the turn of the millennium, this had escalated to over $20 billion, with the industry showing no signs of slowing down. Factoring in online subscriptions, the $40 billion mark was passed by the end of 2008, with projections putting profits from gaming at over $60 billion within another five years.

Where it will end is hard to predict, but it's already fair to call video games the world's most valuable purchased entertainment medium, ahead of Blu-ray and DVD sales, recorded music and cinema box office receipts. In 2008, Nintendo even overtook Google to become the world's most profitable company per employee. Such statistics are a tribute to games' phenomenal appeal, but also to the steady expansion of their demographic: it will be half a century before video games will be truly 'native' to every age group, by which stage the very definition of a video game will have shifted to cover a far broader spectrum of products than it applies to today. Already, analysts and audiences are struggling to keep up with the shifting boundaries of the gaming world, with games increasingly available on every electronic device it is possible to buy: calculators, watches, mobile phones, MP3 players. Yet perhaps the most significant attribute that games possess is their supreme suitability for the digital age.

As the book, newspaper, magazine, music, film and television industries have discovered to their cost, the accelerating migration of consumers towards digital formats is deeply damaging to the profitability of companies that traditionally make the bulk of their money by supplying physical products to retail outlets – and by charging advertisers for the privilege of featuring inside them. A mantra that's often repeated in business is that the price of a product tends towards the cost of distribution, and when the distribution method is the internet, this cost starts to look very close to zero. Games are almost uniquely well placed among media to buck this trend. For a start, they tend to be much more difficult to pirate than other media, given both the degree of copyright protection console manufacturers build into their machines and the sheer size and complexity of most titles compared to text, music or non-interactive moving images. Beyond this, the very way in which games are consumed makes them a very different case to non-interactive media. A brand new mainstream game costs $40 or more, and in return it offers a 'live' experience that cannot simply be reproduced or consumed passively. Games are premium products, and are perceived as such.

The time a player will invest in playing a major new game is typically at least twenty hours, a figure that in the case of multi-player or role-playing games may run into the hundreds or even thousands. This means that ill-made, disposable products simply don't work in the gaming mainstream. The most financially successful console game of all time, *Grand Theft Auto* IV, is designed to take around 100 hours to complete, a tribute to the complexities of its non-linear virtual world. With a budget esti-mated at over $100 million, the game credits a production team of over 550 people, plus almost double that number again of voice actors and performers used for motion-capturing virtual citizens. The result was both a brilliantly realised virtual world and the most successful release of an entertainment product in history. Retailing at $60, GTA IV grossed $500 million in revenues in its first week on sale in April 2008, $310 million of which came on its first day, substantially more than the previous holders for the most successful book (*Harry Potter & The Deathly Hallows* at $220 million in twenty-four hours) and the most successful film (*Spider-Man 3* at $60 million).

Meanwhile, in online gaming, the biggest titles cost around $10 per month to play, and offer different but similarly robust reasons for spending to digital consumers: the fact that the entire point of gaming in a virtual online world is the people you get to play with, and the knowledge that your achievements are both

29

valid and cannot be taken away from you so long as you keep paying your monthly bill. Outside of the official realm of an online game, there is no gaming community to speak of and thus no incentive to invest time or energy in playing something that offers no guarantee of fairness, regular updates, reliability or company. As with GTA IV, the business of building a rewarding and engrossing virtual world from scratch – let alone maintaining it – is extremely labour-intensive, and essential if a consumer's interest is going to be maintained. In this context, the most successful online games rank among the world's most valuable media properties, with the most famous of all – *World of Warcraft* – generating over \$1 billion a year in revenues from over twelve million subscribers.

The story of the gaming industry is, it seems, a remarkable and cloudless tale of expansion, with money virtually making itself for all involved. Even in the advertising sector, where digital revenues across other media have proved unable even to approach the levels of the pre-digital age, the video games market is growing by more than 10 per cent a year, thanks to the hundreds of millions of eyeballs now watching games for hours every day. And yet, when viewed by sector rather than under the umbrella of global statistics, gaming reveals itself to be a rather more complicated and contradictory field than the overarching trends imply.

Much like most other creative sectors, the video games industry is divided between those companies who fund and distribute games, the publishers, and those who actually make them, the developers. It's a divide that exists for sensible historical reasons.

Funding, sales and distribution expertise don't tend to coincide with creative and production skills, although the giant companies of the gaming world – Sony, Nintendo, Sega, Electronic Arts and others – encompass both publishing and development divisions. The industry also consists of two parallel sectors: games on consoles, and games on computers. Computers are a constantly evolving field, but consoles advance in sudden leaps: since the 1980s, an entirely new generation of machines has arrived approximately every six years, each time bringing with it a wilder rush of growth followed by relative decline. Given the increasingly vast amounts of capital required to develop a next-generation console, this cyclical pressure has over time made the games industry both volatile and highly reliant – among mainstream publishers – on coming up with hit titles, whose revenues offset the increasingly huge up-front costs of hardware and software development.

In the first few years of the twenty-first century, there were genuine fears that the mainstream games industry was becoming a victim of its own success, crushed under the weight of escalating budgets and consumer expectations, with profit margins actually shrinking and publishers becoming increasingly risk-averse. The price of a major game failing after a year or more of development and the expenditure of a seven- or eight-digit sum could easily be bankruptcy. As the CEO of one of Britain's largest independent games developers explained to me, 'the costs of making a big game have escalated faster than sales in the shops. Sales go up 15 per cent a year, but creation goes up 25 per cent. That means it is very difficult now to make a game that sells enough to be profitable.' Gaming was at once an over-invested, dazzling and yet strangely constricted world.

Digital distribution has since begun to transform this situation, opening the floodgates to smaller and more innovative projects by allowing games to be sold directly to their audience online rather than through the expensive, marketing-intensive and extremely limiting arena of retail outlets. Despite games' numerous natural advantages as media in a digital era, however, it's far from the case that companies across the industry have simply breathed a collective sigh of relief and begun to make a fortune online. For a start, although their products may be digitally robust in comparison to print or music, the business model of most major publishers still relies on the most conventional of twentieth-century tactics: selling boxed products out of shops, backed up with multi-million-dollar advertising campaigns and quasi-monopolistic distribution networks. Now that even minor competitors are able to sell directly to consumers online, many of the biggest games publishers around are facing the paradoxical situation of a hugely successful industry within which their own financial exposure and levels of risk are higher than ever.

Digital distribution has ushered in a whole new class of medium-priced ($5 to $20) titles with less glossy production than the biggest budget titles, but far more scope for experiment and, often, old-fashioned gaming fun: good news for consumers, and for levels of creativity in the industry as a whole, but bad news for companies for whom such offerings won't be able to replace the kind of income generated by an old-fashioned boxed sale.

While consoles remain by far the most valuable sector of gaming for the moment, it's above all on the open internet that gaming's future is taking shape. And, for all the success of the mid-priced movement, this is looking increasingly like a tale of two extremities. At one end are the makers of virtual worlds – companies creating realms that millions of people can enter, embodying themselves in virtual alter egos and struggling to attain virtual items and achievements within an entirely absorbing context. At the other end, though, is perhaps a more unexpected class of game that draws as much inspiration from the industry's very early days as it does from the glittering prospect of ever-more-advanced technologies. This is what is known as the causal or 'independent' gaming sector, a field that is enjoying more growth in terms of actual games and users than the rest of the industry combined.

Casual games tend only to cost a couple of dollars, or even to be made available for free and make their profits via a combination of advertising, micro-payments and one-off charges for various kinds of premium access. It's a model that owes everything to the internet, but that has itself rapidly become one of the greatest engines of online innovation around, not to mention a magnet for an entire generation of ambitious young programmers, designers, and even writers and artists.

One of the most influential of all casual gaming companies is Playfish, a firm that has devoted itself to the social side of these games. Specifically, Playfish makes games that can be played via the social networking site Facebook, which in 2009 had more than 200 million active users worldwide; a total set to increase to over half a billion by the end of 2010. The games themselves are simple, but beautifully done: a geography quiz, a series of word puzzles, a game where you look after a cute pet, a four-part intelligence test called *How Big is Your Brain*? But the social integration they offer is subtle and extremely powerful, seamlessly integrating with users' Facebook accounts so that they can instantly keep track of – and attempt to better – their friends' scores, or admire each other's pets. And behind it all lies a network of data analysis and tracking that sets a global standard not just for gaming, but for anyone hoping to make money from media in a digital world.

Playfish's CEO, Kristian Segerstråle, has a successful background in game design for mobile phones. Yet, as he explained to me at Playfish's London office in mid-2009, the scale of success that Playfish has experienced had caught him by surprise. 'It's fair to say that we have been overwhelmed. We started off eighteen months ago with four of us. We are well over 100 people now in four offices: China, America, London, Norway. Our games have been installed nearly 80 million times globally. We have around 30 million monthly players. Our first game, launched in December 2007, has had more than half a billion game plays since then.' By contrast, the most popular video on YouTube (founded in 2005) has been played around 120 million times, more than four times fewer.

Social and casual gaming offers not only a new model of tapping consumer demand, i.e. integration with social networks, but, more importantly for the industry as a whole, a radical new way of thinking about games as a media service rather than merely a product. 'With a social game,' Segerstråle explains, 'you only invest a fraction of the total development cost in the pre-launch, because you want to get it out as soon as possible. You don't have a separate publisher or a crazy crunch at the end to deliver a huge project on a set date. What you want to do is get something out and get a sense of how big it might be. If it's a dog, you should kill it as soon as possible. If it turns out to be a success, you add more.' Gone are the massive – and massively risky – up-front investments. The majority of spending occurs instead after a title has launched, and can thus be based on direct feedback from and observation of users' habits.

It is, Segerstråle acknowledges, a model that has a lot in common with the web industry, 'where people are incredibly used to the idea of tracking traffic through a site and optimising it'. And the data generated by playing a game – an interactive process far more complicated than the use of any other website, that might involve many hundreds of actions and reactions with mouse and keyboard within the space of a few minutes – yields insights into users' behaviours that are far beyond any conventional online analytic tools. Playfish itself tracks over 100 million data points every day, giving it a fantastically detailed real-time picture of exactly how all its games are being played: information that it can follow up with targeted email surveys, asking individual players why they behaved in a particular way.

Like other creative media, though, the most important single variable between any online game and its users is something less easily quantified than efficiency, accuracy or ease of use – enjoyment. An entirely feedback-led product also tends to be a boring product, something that contradicts the entire point of a game. It's a fine balance between creativity and responsiveness that Segerstråle sees as one of the defining features of the games industry in the future – and that other media would do well to attend to. 'The trick is not to get lost in the data. That means figuring out what desirable behaviour is on the part of your players, and the skill set for doing that tends to be quite different from the skill set of dreaming up something original, which is a projection of what you think is right in a game. One big challenge for structuring games companies in the future is going to be finding the right balance between being both creatively led and reacting to data.'

As other media have discovered, the constant feedback that a digital product offers can be as disturbing as it is informative: noting which articles get the most hits and provoke the most comments on a newspaper website is, for instance, not necessarily a good guide to either their quality or the benefits they bring to the company in terms of public perception and willingness to spend. In a data-driven age, however, games are out there on their own in terms of both the quantity and quality of information on players' actions they offer, not to mention the potential sophistication of relationships they offer between fellow players, and between players and the company.

One corner of the Playfish office is devoted to player feedback and, as Segerstråle puts it, 'you'd be amazed at the stuff people send in'. Stuck to the wall are drawings and photographs that people have made of their virtual pets in Playfish's hit game *Pet Society*, including, in one case, a snapshot of a two-foot-high cat knitted out of thick blue yarn. It is, he notes, not what the media conventionally thinks of as a typical gamer's enthusiasm, although it's in fact far more mainstream than most of the violence that tends to dominate press coverage. 'The people who want to blow things up in games are a narrow bunch. What we are doing has a broader appeal. In the past, so much of the game world has been focused on these very male fight-or-flight emotions, really until the Wii it was like this. We recently did a game on Facebook called *Restaurant City*, which is all about working with your friends in a restaurant. It's completely non-traditional, but that title has grown faster than any of our previous games.'

Increasingly, it seems, the games industry has discovered that the most successful games of all are those that come closest to real life, not in terms of ever more expensively produced realistic sounds and images, but in terms of the range of social interactions and opportunities for expression they offer: simple, fundamental things, done well, that are a pleasure to share with friends or while away a few moments on a smart phone during a commute. This is far from the sum total of gaming, but it is its nimblest and fastest-growing sector, and reveals, rather like *Spacewar!* did, the full potential of computing machines, not as isolated marvels, but as interfaces with the human world.

Finally, while it is the players who are the ultimate test of any game's success, it is also the workers who are the test of any industry's vigour. And gaming, here, is enjoying a golden dawn. According to a survey of teen career preferences by MTV, 'video game designer' now tops the league of aspirations, beating astronaut, sports star and actor. The best and the brightest are flocking towards the medium, drawn by its incredible growth and potential for innovation, by its increasing cultural dominance, and by the sheer diversity and creative energy it represents: writers, directors, programmers, producers, actors, artists, animators, engineers and design philosophers all have their place in a successful games company, even if the hours are notoriously long and the risks substantial.

As the world plunges headfirst into the digital revolution, video games are emerging as one of its most significant nexuses: a many-headed, compulsively innovative pool of talent and possibility. Like any other medium, parts of the industry will have to adapt to the changing order of things, or face disaster. But most gaming companies' relationships with their consumers are growing ever closer: it is not only the world's fastest growing medium, but also the fastest growing area of global expertise in how to entertain, retain and connect twenty-first-century consumers. If the future is looking more and more like a game, it's partly because the science of satisfaction has never before been so precise, so powerful, or so profitable. Where play goes, the world will follow.

CHAPTER 4

A beautiful science

A video game's relationship with the world appears to be simple enough, no matter how complex the game: it offers delight and diversion, and does so by simplifying and reconstructing reality in pleasing ways. Behind this, however – and behind the idea of fun with which this book began – lies a particular complexity that holds the key both to games' extraordinary appeal and their extraordinary potential for challenging the ways in which we understand our own relationship with the world.

Take the act of jumping. As many commentators, including Raph Koster, have noted, a great number of games involve jumping as a key aspect of their control system – from Nintendo's *Mario* games (Mario was in fact called 'Jump Man' in the very first game he appeared in, jumping being his defining attribute) to the free-running titles currently taking the console world by storm. It's a mechanism that clearly holds a deep appeal for players. What's remarkable, however, is that the amount of time characters spend in the air while jumping is extremely similar across a huge range of titles.

Why is this remarkable? Because the time taken to jump could, theoretically, be anything that a game designer wants. And yet there is an incredible consistency to the jump time in a whole host of games – and not in any sense that directly echoes reality. The jump time from *Mario* onwards tends, in fact, to be considerably longer than is physically possible: around double the duration of the time that an ordinary human can lift themselves off the ground for. The unspoken gaming consensus is something almost Platonic – an idealised version of the 'right' kind of leap. As this suggests, what we are often seeking in games is not so much an escape from reality as a more perfect, and an infinitely reproducible, version of certain aspects of it.

This perfection is perhaps most clearly visible when it takes on a distinctly unreal form, and one of the most distinctively Platonic forms any game has ever achieved can be found in what would be many people's nomination for the greatest single-player game of all time, *Tetris*. Devised in 1984 by the Russian computer scientist Alexey Pajitnov, *Tetris* features just seven pieces, each composed of four blocks (collectively known as 'tetriminoes'). The player has to fit them together into a perfectly solid structure as they fall one by one down the screen in a random, unending sequence. The only method of control is rotation and horizontal motion. Make a line, and it vanishes; it gets faster over time. That's it. And yet this simple creation has outsold the biggest movie blockbusters, made more money than the most expensive artworks, and accounted for more human hours than even the most compelling soap operas, thanks to 70 million global sales of the original and several times as many sales again of its clones, sequels and variations.

In a sense, Pajitnov didn't so much invent *Tetris* as discover it. The game is based on an ancient Roman puzzle involving pieces composed of five squares (known as *pentominos*), itself based on Greek and other more ancient forms of play. Crucially, though, *Tetris* translated a sophisticated mathematical recreation into real time and into the tiny universe of a computer, where score can be kept and pieces thrown at the player in an endless stream. It's a perfect demonstration of the ability of digital media to give an unprecedented form to a very ancient human fascination; and to generate the kind of complexity that in the days before computers could only come from locking horns with another person.

Why, though, is *Tetris*'s brand of complexity quite so enjoyable? Part of the answer lies, once again, in its combination of great sophistication with immaculate simplicity. You can work out how to play *Tetris* in seconds. But the challenge it represents is not just hard, but fiendish. Mathematically speaking, it's known as an NP-hard problem (which stands for a 'non-deterministic polynomial hard' problem). In practice this means that there is no way of 'solving' *Tetris* in any conceivable amount of time by generalising from a set of rules. The optimum way to play can only be understood by an exhaustive analysis of every possible move available at any particular moment in time. The significance of presenting such a complex problem so accessibly is in the degree to which it raises the boredom threshold of a player (the free game *Minesweeper*, which comes bundled with copies of Microsoft Windows, is also an NP-hard problem). Playing *Tetris* is a mathematically endless undertaking. You can never say you have mastered it in terms of exhausting its possibilities: you can only improve your tactics. Moreover, it is a mathematical inevitability that even the greatest player is eventually doomed to lose.

Here, in its simplest form, is gaming's most fundamental point: what satisfies us most may be easy to grasp, but it must not be easy to master or complete. And the perfect way to produce this moment-by-moment level of complexity is the constant feedback and interaction that a game environment can give; something that is almost like a living thing in its shifting, ceaseless demands on our attention.

Complexity is only part of the *Tetris* equation. There's also what Pajitnov himself called the 'emotional dynamic' of the game – the rhythmic, visual pleasure that arises, with practice, as you successfully slot piece after piece into place. It's a sensation lodged somewhere between auto-hypnosis and an almost preternaturally satisfying kind of comprehension, a state combining immersion and responsiveness that was given a name in the 1970s by the Hungarian psychologist Mihaly Csikszentmihalyi that's used to this day. He called it 'flow'.

Flow, Csikszentmihalyi argued, was the kind of mental state that was experienced by a top athlete executing a perfect sequence of manoeuvres or a musician losing themselves completely in the performance of a piece; a way of acting in response to constant, shifting stimuli that represented 'optimal experience'. It's a state of harmony to which most forms of play aspire, and in many ways provides a perfect metaphor for the balance of rules, actions and consequences that all video game designers hope to build into their virtual worlds – a state that itself evidences our absorption and pleasure.

All of which may begin to sound more than a little mystical – and more than a little odd too, in the context of a medium whose every component is demonstrably either a zero or a one lodged somewhere in the matrix of a machine's memory. And yet, if you actually talk to anyone about why they play video games, it won't be long before notions of escape, wonder, self-expression and narrative immersion begin to float to the surface. As I discovered in my very first encounter with the text-based world of the most primitive games of the 1980s, my mind was very quick to project itself – and a version of me – imaginatively into the other world of the machine. It was like falling down a rabbit hole, or stepping out of the back of an ordinary wardrobe into a winter forest. And this combination of projection and wonder is something that many students of game design take extremely seriously.

Intriguingly, the standard term now used to describe a person's presence within a video game is one borrowed not from narratives (i.e. a 'character' or 'protagonist') but from mythology: an *avatar*. The word is taken directly from Sanskrit, and features prominently in Hindu mythology. Its translation in English is usually 'incarnation' but, more literally, it means 'descent', and implies the process by which a higher spiritual being takes on mortal flesh. It is a word that historically has been used to describe the great heroes of Indian myth and legend, for instance Rama, hero of the epic *Ramayana*, or Krishna, hero of the *Bhagavad Gita* and *Bhagavata Purana*.

This may sound a thousand miles away from what happens when you start to play on a computer. And yet in many ways it's hard to find a more evocative description of one central aspect of the game-playing experience than this notion of embodi-ment. It's also something that has recently been high-lighted by James Cameron's $200 million film *Avatar* (2009). In this science fiction epic an injured US marine is given new life in an alien world by the transference of his mind into a specially bred alien body. It's a futuristic fantasy that's very much of our time, exploring the degree to which technology promises not only the enhancement of our existing lives, but the possibility of entirely new kinds of existence, and even of entirely new worlds.

Avatar is a fable about the fascination these possibilities exert, and the degree to which embodying a person in a separate avatar can blur their sense of reality and of what it means to be human. The central character, Jake, ends up shifting his allegiance from the humanity of his original body to the alien race whose planet he finds himself on. It's also, incidentally, a film whose creative process itself embodied a blurring of real and fictional worlds, thanks to the use of a 'virtual camera', which allowed the director to see in real time the digitally constructed characters and envi-ronments that his real actors' performances were being modelled onto. As Cameron put it in an interview with the *New York Times*, 'It's like a big, powerful game engine. If I want to fly through space, or change my perspective, I can. I can turn the whole scene into a living miniature.'

Such blurring has long been a reality in the world of video gaming, which itself draws deeply on the realms of science fiction and fantasy for inspiration. Between 1978 and 1980, a two-man team designed the first true virtual world – the very first 'place' hosted on a machine within which multiple people could interact. It was, for them, a natural enough decision to make it a place corresponding to the established universe of fantasy role-playing games – of swords, sorcery, dark forests and mysterious caves. This is the place from which almost all modern virtual worlds descend, and in many ways the very familiarity of its details is liable to overshadow the radicalism of its conception.

One of these men was Roy Trubshaw, a graduate student at the University of Essex; the other was Richard Bartle, a fellow student one year Trubshaw's junior, and now a professor himself at Essex. The virtual world itself was a text-only zone they called MUD (for Multi-User Dungeon) and, as Bartle explained to me, the motivation behind its creation was unapologetically ambitious. 'What I wanted to do was make worlds. I wanted to make places that people could visit. Because when you visit a place that isn't in the real world you can be yourself in ways you can't in the real world.'

Here was a logical next step beyond the thought-experiments that the last hundred years had so far been conjuring in fiction, from H G Wells to J G Ballard via J R R Tolkien: putting real people into a make-believe place, and seeing what stories they themselves would enact. It was a development, Bartle noted, that took some getting used to, and required a little ingenuity on his part to draw out his student volunteers. 'I introduced a female character into the game, to give them the idea of pretending. She was played by me. It wasn't that I was pretending to be a woman: I was just playing a character who was female. And other people then began to realise that they could pretend to be what they were not. And the idea was that, eventually, they might then realise that they themselves were someone who they might not otherwise have realised they could be.'

It's here that the semi-mystical idea of embodiment begins to come into its own. As Bartle explained, the underlying notion of what people want from a 'true' virtual world is something that closely mirrors an anthropological idea known as the 'hero's journey'. It's a phrase taken from the work of the twentieth-century American mythologist Joseph Campbell who, from his studies of comparative mythology, formulated a pattern that he saw as the fundamental structure of almost every heroic myth through history from around the world. The details of the pattern are complex, but in outline it's simple enough. The hero is called to adventure; he or she crosses the threshold from the mundane world into the world of adventure; is given knowledge, then is tested and tempted; confronts a nemesis; and then journeys back to the old world once again, transformed by experience. In modern times, *Star Wars* conforms pretty perfectly to the pattern – and, indeed, George Lucas drew explicitly on Campbell's work while writing the screenplays.

The hero's journey is a pattern Bartle believes video games aspire to, and for reasons that are in essence mythic, or at least related to a human hunger for particular imaginative forms and kinds of experience. 'The virtual world you go to is this strange new place you must discover. And the first thing you have is this road of trials where you try to find your feet. Then you gain knowledge; you are tempted and tested; and so on, until at the end players gradually stop because the realm has lost its mystical significance. And this corresponds to the end of the plot.' It's a strange, poetic idea, and yet it gets to the heart of something quietly radical about gaming as a medium: its hold on the human imagination, and its ability to make you into the hero of any number of astounding – or modest – stories. The appeal is the sense of wonder that is conjured, but also the need for a kind of security; for, like any myth, the well-designed game always works out in the end, and will always remain there should you feel the urge to return.

The idea of game-playing as a journey is also telling in another sense: because it allows us to think about player motivations in a remarkably precise way. According to Bartle, it's possible to model a player's basic motivations according to a four-part scheme, one divided into the fairly self-explanatory categories of Killer, Achiever, Explorer and Socialiser. These labels describe people's attitude towards both the virtual world and the people and objects within it. A killer is motivated by the urge to act on other characters, violently. An explorer likes to interact with the game world itself, trying to unravel all its secrets. An achiever is driven by the desire to improve their own character and identity, trying to garner as much power, reputation and wealth as possible. And a socialiser interacts with other characters, trying to gain social capital above all.

Nobody is just one thing, of course; and Bartle's system has gained sufficient global weight and reputation that it's now not unheard of for gamers to talk about their 'Bartle quotient', which rates a player on a scale of zero to 100 in each of Bartle's four categories (and isn't allowed to total over two hundred). It may sound bizarre, yet one version of the 'Bartle Test of Gamer Psychology' maintained by the site gamerDNA has now been taken by almost 600,000 people worldwide. My own results class me as 87 per cent achiever, 53 per cent killer, 40 per cent explorer and just 20 per cent socialiser – and are an uncannily accurate snapshot of my gaming style, given my distinctly combat-and-acquisition-orientated methods in most of the titles I play.

Bartle believes that players generally remain dominated by one type of motivation throughout their gaming lives. Yet it's possible to trace the path of a player's development through the shifting balance of these motivations over time in a trajectory that mirrors the hero's journey. 'We noticed early on that people follow certain patterns when they start to play. They might first try to kill each other; then they would go off and try to explore the area; then they would spend ages getting points and progressing; and then they would start to spend their time sitting around chatting.' Underlying this is something that combines the imaginative projection of myth with the intense immersion of a sporting or musical performance. As Bartle puts it, 'If you play an MMO, you are the hero. It's not vicarious, it is actually you.

By playing the game, you don't want to have to conform to other people's notions in the real world.'

Bartle's model of player motivations is a powerful way of describing the essential ways that people tend to interact with games worlds – and how, in a well-made game, these priorities shift over time. Similarly, Raph Koster's emphasis on the fundamental relationship between learning, fun and the human mind illuminates some of the biggest 'whys' of gaming with persuasive clarity. When it comes to being bluntly empirical, however, there is perhaps no one better to turn to than Nicole Lazzaro, the founder and president of the player experience and research company XEODesign and a woman with almost twenty years of experience advising everyone from Electronic Arts to the Cartoon Network about how exactly one can describe what's going on in the mind of someone playing a video game.

Lazzaro's research focuses on what she calls the 'role of emotion in games' and, in particular, on those emotions unique to the gaming experience. One of the most important studies her company has undertaken was in 2004, when they took thirty adult gamers and collected three types of data from them based on a gaming session of 90 to 120 minutes. The data consisted of forty-five hours' worth of video recordings, detailed player questionnaires, and a record of thousands of verbal and non-verbal emotional cues (such as facial expressions) recorded during play. What it revealed was a scheme she describes as the 'Four Keys to releasing emotions during play'.

Like Bartle, Lazzaro notes that 'both players and games vary in how important each key is to having fun'. Yet, she continues, the best-selling games – and the best-made games, which are very often the ones selling the most copies – almost all provide substantial emotion in at least three of the four key areas within her scheme, a sure sign that what most satisfies when it comes to gaming is a layering of very particular complexities (and that, when it comes to fun, it's extremely difficult to pull the wool over consumers' eyes).

First among these four key areas is what Lazzaro calls 'hard fun'. This is, in essence, the overcoming of obstacles: the pursuit of a goal, the rewarding of progress and the presence of compelling challenges that demand sophisticated strategies. As you might expect, then, the second key is what's called 'easy fun', which she summarises as 'the sheer enjoyment of experiencing the game', feeding into a player's curiosity, sense of awe and appetite for mystery. This is about a world being engrossing and rich, enticing a player into thinking about it as more than merely an abstract sequence of challenges and propositions. Here, interestingly, even the driest of games like *Tetris* appeared to benefit hugely from subtle details: music, sound effects, distinctive graphical and design features. Immersion, Lazzaro emphasises, is not so much about building meticulous three-dimensional worlds as about surprising and delighting players with the sense of a well-crafted environment with an element of ambiguity and tantalising incompleteness to it.

Then there's the third key, known as 'altered states', formulated in response to players' repeated reports that they enjoyed the way that playing a video game could change how they felt inside. In particular, this relates to how the best games' brand of 'flow' could clear the mind, banish boredom and impart a sense of achievement. And finally, the fourth key comes under the broadest and arguably the most important heading of all, 'the people factor'. A large number of gamers, Lazzaro noted, talk specifically about the enjoyment of playing with others both inside and outside the game. Moreover, she noted, 'what surprised us most was the dramatic contrast in emotional displays between one versus several people playing together. Players in groups emote more frequently and with more intensity than those who play on their own. Group play adds new behaviours, rituals and emotions.' And, of course, the same applies again in a some-what different manner to the complexities of remote play with others – especially when, as is increasingly the case, these remote interactions take place through microphones, speakers and real-time conversation as well as in-game interactions.

In a sense, given the increasing ubiquity of video game-playing and the sheer diversity of games out there, what's surprising is not so much that people play games for many different reasons as the fact that many of these reasons are so fundamentally inter-connected or even identical. As Lazzaro has observed, taking pleasure in feelings of challenge and absorption is pretty much universal. So, too, is the capacity of games to relax and to remove gamers from many real world concerns and, in Bartle's terms, to take them in each other's company along a path of self-expression and experiential thrills that no other recreation offers to anything like the same degree. Then there's also the symbolic, even atavistic, pull of many aspects of games: our innate yearnings, manifesting themselves in these marvellously clever, intense miniature worlds. These are places able to offer a purity and intensity of order and reward that is both lifelike and something life itself cannot habitually deliver in the same degree of concentration.

As I'll be exploring in the next two chapters, in all of these aspects lie both real and imagined dangers for the increasingly substantial percentage of humanity who class themselves as gamers. There's something else, too, that perhaps comes closer to the idea of art than any other kind of satisfaction it's possible for games to offer: the sheer, changeless otherness of gaming, and its strange relationship with passing time. To enter into the world of a game is to visit somewhere unfallen and ageless, where what you do and experience seems to occupy a special, separate kind of temporality; and where the passage of time in your own life leaves no mark. This is true of all art and media to some extent. Yet returning to a favourite book, piece of music or even film brings with it to some extent the changed context of the world and reshapes what you feel on each viewing. The world of a video game, in contrast, is its own context, and is uniquely transporting – one of the reasons why the video game nostalgia industry is already a vast industry all on its own just a few decades on from the birth of the medium itself.

Games are not just other worlds. They can also be, in their way, little Edens; and the incremental thrill of coming to know and to master one has a compelling counterpart in this – the fact that one solved, minute part of the universe will always be there, should you wish to experience it again. It's at once regressive and wonderfully enabling. For many people, as they get older and find that the world around them is increasingly complicated and packed with uncertainties, the existence of some other place over which they have complete control and to which they can always return is one of the most powerful motivators of all.

CHAPTER 5

Dangerous playground

For about as long as new media for communication and representation have been coming into existence, people have been worrying about their impact on both mental and physical health. And they've been doing so for centuries in quite astonishingly similar ways. Compare and contrast, for example, the following three critiques. Number one:

> It gives its disciples not truth, but only the semblance of truth; they will be hearers of many things and will have learned nothing; they will appear to be omniscient and will generally know nothing.

Number two:

> It is a pastime of illiterate, wretched creatures who are stupefied by their daily jobs, a machine of mindlessness

and dissolution. It requires no effort, raises no ideas, raises no questions ...

And number three:

They become like blinking lizards, motionless, absorbed, only the twitching of their hands showing they are still conscious. [It] teaches them nothing. It stimulates no ratiocination, discovery or feat of memory.

Each new medium is being criticised for encouraging various kinds of intellectual laziness. It is also being criticised for doing so in people other than the complainant: each author is concerned with the mental health of 'them', a more vulnerable order of person than they themselves; the new medium seems in each case to offer 'them' a perilous, even sinful, amount of ease. There is an appealing 'semblance' of something meaningful; but underneath that glistening surface there is no real content and nothing of value. There is no 'wisdom' or 'ratiocination' to be found within.

The authors of these critiques are separated by over 2,000 years. The first is from ancient Greece, and is taken from Plato's *Phaedrus*, written around the fourth century BC. In this passage, the character of Socrates is explaining why the written word is dangerously inferior to the practice of spoken debate with another person – because it encourages mere knowledge without understanding. The second critique was published in 1930, and comes from the cantankerous pen of the French author Georges

Duhamel, who argued in his book, *Scenes from the Life of the Future*, against the evils of the new medium of film. And the third comes from a British politician, the Conservative Member of Parliament and current Mayor of London, Boris Johnson, who used his column in the *Daily Telegraph* in December 2006 to highlight the menace of video games. He went on to explain that they were 'a cause of ignorance and underachievement' because they distracted modern youth from productive activities like reading, turning them instead into 'blinking lizards'.

It's useful to begin with opinions rather than with hard statistics because the two often have very little to do with each other. As is always the case with something disturbingly new, many of the greatest objections to video games as a medium are moral and philosophical rather than simply pragmatic. This isn't to say that these objections are wrong or without a basis in reality, but it does mean that they are likely to be confused and based on incomplete information. This chapter, then, aims to disentangle some of the fears, facts and possibilities surrounding video games. It's not a question of whitewashing them beyond criticism, but it is about the fact that many conventional fears surrounding games are misguided – and that games can also be dangerous in ways that don't tend to make headlines.

Video games are powerful: considerably more so in many ways than either television or film, although not as transforming as the written word. Nevertheless, games have conquered the world much faster than any of these earlier media. Print has been around for a good 560 years, and the written word for 5,000 or so; cinema and recorded music for around 100 years, radio broadcasts for 75 years and television for 50 years. Video games have barely four serious decades on the clock, yet they are already sweeping towards a position of dominance, both financially and in terms of attention and influence.

We should acknowledge that the speed of this transition could itself be dangerous. One of the most obvious points to make about any medium is that it should be used responsibly. Games, in particular, are a kind of playground for the mind, and even among adult users it is important to be able to match safety provisions to the kind of equipment that is being used – a precaution that's doubly true when it comes to children and the young. With video games, as with other areas of life, parents should be aware of and understand what their children are doing. Similarly, the population at large should be educated about this arena's nature and possibilities; and there should be an open and well-informed discussion among policy-makers, consumers and those within the industry, leading to sensible forms of legislation and regulation.

With games, the sheer pace at which the medium has developed has stopped much of this from happening. Things are – gradually – changing, but until recently most parents had little or no idea what was going on when their children played a video game. Equally, those in government and the media had little sense of what a game was like to play, rather than to watch from a distance, and those within the industry felt, rightly enough, that they were operating within a field more or less sealed off from mainstream discourse, where the only meaningful thing to do was to keep their heads down and go on making their products.

All of this has provided both the ideal breeding ground for moral panic and for the widening of the divide between those who play and those who don't. It's a division that is still largely generational. When a medium as new and as rapidly evolving as video games first arrives, there is little ability for different generations to share or learn lessons from one another. On top of this, there's the nature of gaming itself. Even television began as a family medium – something that could be shared. Games, however, began as a relatively esoteric, individual activity: a pursuit where there was no experience to share or advice to pass on. That alienation and incomprehension on both sides should remain comes as no surprise. Perhaps at no other point in peacetime history have an older generation seen their experience and knowledge so decisively outdated within their own lifetimes, and while this is a larger phenomenon, games are an increasingly integral part of it.

It's especially troubling because many of the most profound questions video games raise have yet to be addressed. There is, for instance, the growing problem of how to determine the legal status of actions and transactions within virtual worlds. In some ways, the kinds of legal and ethical questions raised here resemble those seen in medical science. Stem cell research, for instance, is a field where what is technically possible has evolved faster than the growth of the legal and philosophical framework addressing it. What are the ethics of creating, destroying and using human embryos in potentially life-saving medical treatments?

The questions thrown up by games may be considerably less challenging ethically, but they too confront our current laws and cultural frameworks with possibilities far outside the imaginations of legislators even half a century ago. For instance, who owns a character or the objects created by a player within a virtual game world? The answer at the moment is the company hosting the game – yet players are now trading virtual goods for thousands, or even tens of thousands, of real dollars. How can this be regulated, taxed or even legally acknowledged? Intellectual property, similarly, is becoming a tricky issue when players are busily innovating within games in ways that may have substantial external applications: in devising, for example, mathematical systems for the fair division of rewards between a large team of cooperating players; or even when the in-game objects they create start to be treated as works of art, or as informal businesses in their own right (selling virtual in-game items for real money is now a multibillion-dollar global industry). And then there's the question of how 'wrongdoing' within a game can be punished or identified. Virtual theft, deception, exploitation and abuse are exceptionally difficult to prove and can be almost impossible for existing legal systems to punish, especially given the permeability of virtual worlds across national borders. Yet some kind of framework is needed. In the most notorious case to come to light, there has already been a murder in China as the result of an in-game theft. In 2005, one player in Shanghai sold on eBay a virtual sword he had been lent by another (to be precise, it was a 'dragon sabre' from the hugely popular online game *The Legend of Mir 3*). When it transpired that there was no legal basis for the recovery of the item, its original 'owner' took the law into his own hands, confronted the thief, and stabbed him to death for real. Such violence is freakishly rare, but the underlying challenges are not, and the increasing value attached to all manner of objects that simply do not exist in the conventional sense is a destabilising development whose effects have only just begun to be felt.

There is, however, some good news to counterbalance the disturbing notion of video games as a force of disruption and alienation – and this is that the notion of games as something generationally isolating and divisive is rapidly becoming less and less true. Consider demographics: where once gaming was the preserve of adolescent males, players increasingly come from all age groups and from both sexes. According to the Entertainment Software Association of America, the world's largest gaming association, the average American video game player is now thirty-five years old and has been playing games for twelve years, while the average frequent buyer of games is thirty-nine. Moreover, 40 per cent of all players are women, with women over eighteen representing a far greater portion of the game-playing population (34 per cent) than boys aged seventeen or younger (18 per cent).

Much of the recent growth in the value of the gaming industry, too, has been driven by the increased diversity and affluence of its consumer base. The agenda, in other words, is increasingly being set by the concerns of mainstream consumers – what they consider acceptable for their children, what they want to play together, and how they want to play across generations. It's something those predicting a bottomless downward spiral of self-isolating gamers should bear in mind. The generation who first encountered games as children in the 1970s and 1980s are now having children themselves, with whom they wish to play games. Already, there are grandparents playing video games with their grandchildren, a scenario that still sounds mildly outlandish, but that will inevitably become commonplace in years to come.

Arguably the greatest lesson the video games industry has learned over the last decade, in fact, is that its biggest potential for growth lies in games designed not for the kinds of players who comprised the bulk of the market in the 1980s and 1990s – self-identified 'gamers', usually male, who wanted hard-core action and equally hard-core kinds of strategy – but for a far larger emerging market of players for whom gaming means a variety of very different interactive experiences that often resemble nothing so much as a traditional board game or a school sports day.

In practical terms, this has been reflected by the industry very rapidly getting its act together on what must be the least debatable part of the debate on games and safety: the need to protect children, and the regulation of violent content within games. Since its introduction in 2003, a ratings system known as the Pan European Game Information System (PEGI) has been adopted by thirty-two European countries and seems likely to spread still further; while in America a similar system run by the Entertainment Software Rating Board has been in operation since

1994. Most media observers would agree that it has taken some time for these bodies to establish themselves and gain the support of the industry. In this respect, however, increasingly vocal media concerns over the content of games have been a blessing in disguise: gaming has made substantial advances in recent years in ensuring that every major title released is rated, that most retailers will not stock unrated titles, and that advertising is also subject to rating controls. A 2008 Nielsen Games study of gaming in Europe suggested that the ratings are now recognised by over 90 per cent of game consumers.

Produces of online games, meanwhile, are making very considerable efforts to ensure that their products offer strictly controlled environments as far as children and other vulnerable users are concerned. Take, for example, the British company Mind Candy, who produce one of the world's leading online social games for children, *Moshi Monsters* (the game itself involves looking after, and showing off, a virtual pet monster). Its CEO, Michael Smith, is clear in his insistence that ensuring abusive adults and cyberbullies can't take advantage of their game is their highest priority as a company. 'Like most of the industry, we take extreme care over this. Everything that is said between players in the game is viewed in public channels: there is no ability to communicate with anyone privately. We have a team of moderators who look over everything that is said and written in the game; children don't give out their real names, or any personal identifying information.' And what about financial exploitation? 'The game is designed to be played for free, although you can get premium content for about £3 per month. And it's designed to be played with parental input, so children can only play after their parents have separately approved this.' It is, he explains, impossible to pay more than £3 per month to play, and there is no use of what Smith calls the 'ethically more fragile model' of advertising.

Moshi Monsters won a National Parenting Publications Award for its work, but its standards are typical of online games aimed specifically at children, a global market that runs well past the hundred million mark in terms of users. Their business model, after all, relies on both the goodwill of parents and strict adherence to ratings guidelines. As Smith puts it, 'It is frustrating, because people outside of the industry don't understand it. The internet is far more important to younger children than television: it's a no-brainer for the new generation. There are now hundreds of millions of children around the world playing safely online; they're safer there than they are on their way to school or in a playground. We can't and shouldn't give unfiltered access to children: they do need limits, they do need supervision. Every responsible designer needs to be aware of this, and everyone that I've come across is.'

It's a refrain that comes up again and again within the industry: responsible design is about ensuring strict adherence to ratings guidelines, and about knowing your audience. But it's also all about your audience knowing you. As Michael Rawlinson, general manager of the world's longest-established trade association representing video games publishers (the Entertainment and Leisure Software Publishers Association), put it to me: 'There does seem to be a point with video games that parents are seen as having no responsibility, and everything is up to the industry. That is ridiculous. We need to encourage parents, and everyone else, to learn more about gaming and play their part. And I think that is happening, as we see the notion of gaming as part of the family lifestyle becoming normalised.' Some sectors of the games industry are extremely well designed for use by children; others cater for an ever-widening diversity of adult tastes. It's just as misleading to think of all modern games as essentially children's toys as it would be to think of all films as suitable for children.

Despite the almost universal prevalence of age ratings, the relationship between violence in games and violence in life is one debate that's unlikely to die down any time soon. And this is in part because it's something that is only too easy to imagine in terms that go well beyond what we're now used to in other media forms. Consider a game like those in the bestselling *Medal of Honor* series: first-person experiences in which absorbing, interactive environments, realised with ultra-realistic graphics and sounds, evoke warfare in such detail that it can virtually be smelt. The weapons on the screen look and sound exactly like the real things, and are seen as if through the eyes of the soldier a player controls, ducking and diving their way through the campaigns of the Second World War, slaughtering enemies as they go. It's easy enough to understand why this kind of interactive pursuit is seen as a level beyond video-nasties in the corruption-of-youth stakes, and it generates a number of intransigent questions that mustn't be brushed aside even by the most ardent defenders of gaming. What exactly is the relationship between game violence and real-world violence? And is the likelihood that a certain number of inappropriately young people will play certain games so awful that these games should not be allowed to exist?

As far as the first of these questions is concerned, scientific studies can often seem confusing to the point of contradiction, which should come as no surprise to students of any of the media/violence controversies of the past half-century. In 2007, however, one unusually authoritative paper appeared in the peer-reviewed US journal *Psychiatric Quarterly* (entitled 'The Good, the Bad and the Ugly: A Meta-analytic Review of Positive and Negative Effects of Violent Video Games') that provided hitherto unprecedented clarity on the issue. Its author, Dr Christopher John Ferguson, an assistant professor of psychology at Texas A&M International University, set out to compare every article published in a peer-reviewed journal between 1995 and April 2007 that in some way investigated the effect of playing violent video games on some measure of aggressive behaviour. A total of seventeen published studies matched these criteria – and Ferguson's conclusions were unexpectedly unequivocal. 'Once corrected for publication bias,' he reported, 'studies of video game violence provided no support for the hypothesis that violent video game-playing is associated with higher aggression.' Moreover, he added, the question 'do violent games cause violence?' is itself flawed in that 'it assumes that such games have only negative effects and ignores the possibility of positive effects' such as the possibility that violent games allow 'catharsis' of a kind in their players.

This, for many people, is sufficiently radical stuff to provoke considerable scepticism. And, indeed, 2008 saw a rather different case being made by a peer-reviewed longitudinal study of violence in games published in the US journal *Pediatrics*. A joint venture between American and Japanese academics, this paper ('Longitudinal Effects of Violent Video Games on Aggression in Japan and the United States') argued that, across three samples of Japanese and American secondary school pupils examined at two points in time over a period of three to six months, 'habitual violent video game play early in the school year predicted later aggression, even after controlling for gender and previous aggressiveness in each sample'. The authors thus recommended 'reducing the exposure of youth to this risk factor'. What are we to make of contradictions like this?

One nation that already seems to have taken the most radical anti-games school of advice to heart is Germany, where in June 2009 leaders of all sixteen German states voted to ban entirely all games 'where the main part is to realistically play the killing of people or other cruel or inhuman acts of violence against humans or manlike characters'. Germany has always been strict in its regulation of games, and the ban is a direct consequence of the shootings that occurred in a German school in March 2009, when a seventeen-year-old ex-pupil, Tim Kretschmer, killed nine pupils and three teachers before turning the gun on himself. Kretschmer, it was widely reported, spent a large amount of time playing first-person-shooter video games, and there were suggestions that these had somehow 'trained' him to perpetrate the massacre.

The case is, like all such occurrences, a rare and extremely disturbing one. Yet attempts to trace a causal relationship between violent games and real-life killings tend, at best, to be misleading, and at worst simply to be inaccurate scapegoating. Adam Lewitt, writing in *The Sunday Times*, was typical in his description of 'remarkable parallels' between the bestselling game *Far Cry 2* and the killings. 'In the game it is essential to hijack cars to move around,' he explained (which it isn't); 'characters in the game ... wear black camouflage uniforms – the clothing Kretschmer wore' (almost none of them do); 'Most sinister of all, *Far Cry 2*'s killer uses a Beretta 92 handgun, the weapon fired 112 times by Kretschmer' (no Beretta handgun appears in the game); the game 'also rewards players who shoot their victims in the head, the style of killing chosen by Kretschmer' (it doesn't). Perhaps more relevant was the large supply of guns the boy's father kept at home, the fact that his father had been taking him shooting since the age of eight, and his recent depression. But such reasons are less incendiary fuel for speculation.

Although it grabs occasional headlines, the case in favour of video games directly causing violence is one that it's increasingly difficult to take seriously. With over 90 per cent of Western adolescents now playing video games to some degree, it's hard to see how a near-universal pattern of behaviour can, in any meaningful sense, predict a rare occurrence of violent, let alone murderous, behaviour. Moreover, when it comes to the most comprehensive study of high-school shootings ever undertaken (a 2002 study by the US Secret Service and Department of Education, investigating thirty-seven such incidents between 1974 and 2000), it transpires that only 59 per cent of the perpetrators took even 'some interest' in violent media of any kind; and that, among these media, video games were the least significant, with only 12 per cent of subjects expressing an attraction towards them. Even taking into account only the incidents that occurred after 1989, by which year 'violent' games could safely be said to have become widespread, a mere 15 per cent of perpetrators were noted to have shown any interest in violent games.

Of course, more sensible critics of violent games will reply that, while it's largely meaningless to look for a direct causal relationship between violent games and incidents of violent crime, it is reasonable to suppose that an interactive medium that allows people to shoot at other (virtual) people within highly realistic settings may help to create a culture of desensitisation towards violence. It's a theory that's not readily susceptible to either proof or disproof, but it has a ring of common sense to it – something that it shares with the most commonly heard arguments against graphic depictions of violence in any medium. Socially and morally, it is argued, such depictions (and, in the case of games, enactments) have a coarsening effect on their audience – as well as a potentially far more dangerous degree of influence on vulnerable individuals. Is this true?

This feeling of decline may strike an emotional chord with many, but it is hard to bear out statistically. The consumption of video games – including, naturally, violent ones – has increased by several thousand per cent since the start of the 1990s. Yet violent crime in the US, the EU, Canada and Australia has decreased dramatically over this same period. Among the generation who have grown up playing video games in America, rates of violent crime are the lowest in recorded history. Tens of millions of video games are now sold and played each year, compared to none whatsoever fifty years ago, and yet 'gaming' societies have yet to fall into any kind of an abyss – at least as far as violence is concerned.

Is there, nevertheless, an aesthetic and moral case to be made for the banning of violent and explicit media? In one sense, versions of the same case have been made for the last century or more – against novels, comic books, rock music, and indeed against almost anything that seeks to represent aspects of life and society that some people view as shameful, undesirable, antisocial or corrupting. The case for age restrictions, and for restrictions on some extremities of content, is one that all sides are willing to concede and debate. So far as censorship in general is concerned, however, one of the most eloquent and definitive ripostes to the notion that society has a duty to censor violent media was given by Judge Richard A Posner in his 2001 ruling on an Indianapolis city ordinance that had sought to restrict children's access to violent arcade games. 'To shield children right up to the age of eighteen from exposure to violent descriptions and images would not only be quixotic, but deforming,' declared Posner. 'It would leave them unequipped to cope with the world as we know it. Maybe video games are different. They are, after all, interactive. But this point is superficial, in fact erroneous. All literature (here broadly defined to include movies, television and the other photographic media, and popular as well as highbrow literature) is interactive; the better it is, the more interactive. Literature when it is successful draws the reader into the story, makes him identify with the characters, invites him to judge them and quarrel with them, to experience their joys and sufferings as the reader's own ... It is conceivable that pushing a button or manipulating a toggle stick engenders an even deeper surge of aggressive joy, but of that there is no evidence at all.'

To deny the link between games and violence in society is not, however, to say that gaming is a medium without its hazards. For, despite its headline-grabbing potential, it's not the research on violence that gets to one of the most troubling aspects of video games. For this, we must look to a far more statistically robust phenomenon – and one not only disapproving social watchdogs but also gamers themselves acknowledge as one of their pastime's greatest hazards: addiction.

The word 'addiction' itself is a loaded one. For many people, it conjures images of physical, mental and moral decline; of gaunt figures hungering for their next fix, less than fully in control of their own lives and minds. It's an image that doesn't much resemble most people's experience of video gaming. Yet almost anyone who has played games at all seriously will acknowledge that their compelling nature – and the problematic relationship some users have with this – raises a number of questions that cannot easily be dismissed.

There have already been several attempts to define 'video games addiction' as a psychological condition, including an effort to have it admitted to the latest edition of the Diagnostic and Statistical Manual of Mental Disorders (DSM), the definitive global guide to mental health. This effort was abandoned due to a lack of evidence, but considerable research continues in the field, with the comparison to other behavioural addictions and compulsive behaviours – from gambling to shopping – shedding some light on the more extreme end of the spectrum. Contrary to the claims of some critics, however, playing video games is categorically not analogous to taking drugs or drinking to excess. While a game may be said to act like a drug in the compelling pleasure it gives, the behavioural mechanics of gaining pleasure from games are the very opposite of the passive process of ingesting a substance and waiting for it to act. It is action, coupled with challenges, incentives and constant feedback, that makes gaming what it is.

Action is, of course, itself a double-edged sword. The most 'addictive' games tend to be those that are most rewardingly complex, the most skilfully designed to engage and reward their users. In fact, many critics theorise, they are so good at doing this that the resulting pleasure tends dangerously towards the pathological. Players become so engaged in the constant inter-actions and stimuli offered by a video game that they are effec-tively drugged by their own brains into a state of imbalance, potentially neglecting other aspects of their 'real' lives to a dangerous degree. This hypothesis that has been explored by expert critics like the British neurologist Susan Greenfield as part of her analysis of children's use of computers and the internet in her book *iD: The Quest for Identity in the 21st Century*. According to Greenfield, excessive dopamine production induced by onscreen stimulation may in the long term reduce the acti-vation of an area of the brain known as the prefrontal cortex, in the process making people less empathetic, more self-centred, and generally more addictive and immature as personalities. It's a trend that may augur, Greenfield suggests, 'a world arguably trapped in early childhood, where the infant doesn't yet think metaphorically'.

Greenfield's concerns are offered in strict scientific terms but they embody a far more ancient and atavistic class of human fear: that people are perilously drawn by temptation to withdraw from real life's complexities into a solipsistic, simpler world. In the case of video games, in particular, it's hard to deny this kind of escape isn't a large part of their appeal. Escape, simplification and control play their part in all games, and in electronic games have reached a remarkable pitch of sophistication. Yet how can they be both ethically and emotionally crude in comparison to other media, so that to play them is to risk permanent infantalisation, while at the same time being devilishly sophisticated? Entertaining people not with drug-based stimulations, tempting cash prizes and high stakes, or sex and violence, but with satisfying symbolic challenges and tests of skill is a incredibly complex task, after all. At what point, moreover, does this cease to be entertainment and become a solid curse?

One of the most intriguing studies in this area is a paper entitled 'Pathological Video Game Use among Youth 8 to 18: A National Study', published by Dr Douglas A Gentile in 2008 in the US journal *Psychological Science*. The criteria Gentile used to discuss pathological game-playing were based on the DSM criteria for pathological gambling – which, being a behavioural addiction, offered a far more pertinent comparison to games than the idea of substance abuse. Gentile's method was to assess responses to a Harris poll of 1,178 Americans aged between eight and eighteen, taken in January 2007, according to eleven 'indicators' based on the DSM criteria for problem gambling. When, he argued, an individual had six or more positive responses out of the eleven categories, this suggested they might have an unhealthy relationship with video games.

Gentile's questions included whether gamers felt restless or irritable when attempting to cut down their gaming, whether schoolwork or chores were being skipped in order to play, and whether respondents found it necessary gradually to increase the amount of time they spent playing games in order to keep on experiencing the same level of satisfaction from them. His results, he emphasised, were not testing whether people played games 'too much' in terms of raw hours spent in front of a machine. They were intended, rather, to distinguish between merely engaging with games, and developing a problematic relationship with them.

The results were striking. Among those respondents who were video game-players, 8.5 per cent met six or more of the 'pathological' criteria. These weren't the people who played the games the most, or those who were most deeply engaged by individual games, but they were, Gentile noted, 'twice as likely as non-pathological gamers to have been diagnosed with an attention problem'. Moreover, he concluded, 'these results confirm that pathological gaming can be measured reliably' and 'that it is not simply isomorphic with [that is, essentially identical to] a high amount of play'.

Many gamers and industry representatives leapt to criticise the study, which certainly had its limitations (including the fact that, because the original survey was an 'opt-in' questionnaire posted online, the results can't be construed as nationally representative in any sense). Then there were the questions themselves, which have a very different resonance when applied to children playing games at home as opposed to adults spending money on gambling. What child wouldn't answer 'yes' to the question 'Have you played video games as a way of escaping from problems or bad feelings?' or admit to 'skipping their homework' sometimes in order to play a favourite game?

Yet the questions Gentile raises deserve serious consideration. As he pointed out in a subsequent interview with the website Negative Gamer, games are specifically designed to exert the kind of appeal that, in the case of some individuals, can become pathological. 'If you play a game and it doesn't affect you, what do you call it? Boring. You want to be affected, so don't pretend they don't affect you. And that's what most gamers who get really defensive are doing. They're telling this little lie. Games don't affect me, but of course they only want to play games that do affect them.' It's a point that both the games industry and gamers are often unhelpfully evasive in confronting.

The term 'addiction' isn't just emotionally loaded: it also represents a great deal of ambivalence amongst game-players and creators. As a young gamer, I was an avid consumer of magazines that reviewed video games. Reviews tended to be broken down by criteria like the quality of graphics, sound and control systems. But another key rating was always a game's 'addictiveness' – essentially, how much you wanted to go on playing, and how hard you found it to put the controller down and turn the system off. The more of this they had, the better. You wanted, as Gentile puts it, a game to 'affect' you. You didn't, of course, set out to distort your life in a pathological way. But, given how good gaming is at tapping into some very powerful human responses, you couldn't always remain in what felt like total control.

There's an element of this in all popular entertainment. A book is described as 'impossible to put down', and this is high praise. A television series is described as 'compulsive viewing' and this – a term borrowed from a behavioural disorder – is a testament to its quality and the skill of its makers. Yet most people don't worry that books or television series are, of themselves, so appealing that they represent a hazard to consumers. When my parents caught me on numerous occasions reading a favourite book under the covers of my bed at night by torchlight, they may have lightly scolded me, but they didn't feel the need to consult a psychologist about my alarming book addiction. And nor, to be fair, did they worry excessively when there were sporadic rows about how much I should or shouldn't be allowed to play *Zelda* II: *The Adventure of Link* on my Nintendo Entertainment System.

Why, then, the special concerns over games? The basis of this is the idea that they are uniquely powerful as a medium; that, as critics like Susan Greenfield suggest, they simply affect us more, and more dangerously, than pretty much anything else. Yet neurology, even while it explains the precise mechanics of certain feelings, is often an extremely poor guide to social behaviours; and it's certainly safe to say that the reasons people play games pathologically are *never* as simple as 'the game was too powerful for me to handle'. Putting it another way, there is no such thing as a game with which most players have a pathological relationship. As Gentile himself pointed out, the amount of time spent on a game does not correlate with pathological play; and the very idea that games simply act like a mind drug on a hapless minority of their consumers offers little succour to those who do experience these problems, and little in the way of insight or practical advice to everyone else.

Perhaps most tellingly, as the idea of pathological gaming has begun to be taken seriously, the emphasis has increasingly fallen on the social context rather than on the medium itself. In 2006, to much media fanfare, the Smith & Jones Centre launched itself in Amsterdam as the first European institution specifically set up to treat video games addiction. The programme would operate along the lines of previously successful approaches to dealing with behavioural addictions like gambling. Here, surely, was clear evidence that video games were a special, problematic case as a medium.

In November 2008, however, the same clinic made a striking announcement. On the evidence of the hundreds of cases it had treated since opening, the media were told, it would be abandoning the 'addiction' style of treatment for something essentially social and educative in approach. As its founder and head, Keith Bakker, told the BBC, 'These kids come in showing some kind of symptoms that are similar to other addictions and chemical dependencies. But the more we work with [them] the less I believe we can call this addiction . . . Eighty per cent of the young people we see have been bullied at school and feel isolated. Many of the symptoms they have can be solved by going back to good old-fashioned communication.' It was, Bakker explained, a question of understanding why and how they chose to play: 'If I continue to call gaming an addiction it takes away the element of choice these people have.' Once again, the issue is causality and experience had shown that pathological game-playing was itself more of a symptom than a cause of distress.

This doesn't mean that the children going to the centre didn't have real problems that were manifesting in their gaming, or that they hadn't developed some extremely negative and counter-productive gaming habits. But it does suggest that by far the most useful approach is a pragmatic one that overlaps with more general risk and protection factors, rather than one that treats game-playing as an isolated and uniquely perilous pursuit. Some people are psychologically more at risk of developing pathological behaviours than others; some people are more socially at risk than others. Identifying and offsetting these risk factors is vital, but this, as Bakker himself strongly argued, is above all a task for families, schools and gamers themselves to learn about in the broad context of living a psychologically well-balanced life.

In this context, we shouldn't forget that video games actually have an awful lot going for them as a social outlet. You can lose time to games, but it's extremely difficult to lose your health or your wealth to them. Far from being the root of people's problems, many games and their associated communities can provide an excellent mechanism for identifying and supporting those suffering from depression, alienation and other social problems, by functioning as a communications network that reaches many people and places that more conventional pastoral care simply doesn't reach. As Gentile's own report notes, 'it is certainly possible that pathological gaming causes poorer school performance etc., but it is equally likely that children who have trouble at school seek to play games to experience feelings of mastery, or that attention problems cause both poorer school performance and an attraction to games'. Games potentially provide a constant source of information and contact for such people. Compare this to a cable television company where, no matter how many solitary hours someone chooses to spend slumped in front of their screen, the company themselves will have no way of either knowing or doing anything about their behaviour.

Indeed, working on the practical assumption that a minority with unhappy or unbalanced lives are always going to exist to some degree, and are always going to look to something for comfort and escape, games start to seem one of the most benign – and effective – options they could select. It's said that the devil makes work for idle hands. But the world has found few better cures for mental idleness than video games. In an ideal world, everyone would enjoy from birth an attentive, close-knit family; safe, efficient public transport and access to pleasant outdoor spaces and social facilities; they would socialise with a group of close friends living within easy visiting distance and so on. In the inevitable absence of much of this for many people, however, games can become important for a huge number of positive reasons; and even those who use them to escape or evade bigger issues in their lives may be doing something entirely reasonable in the circumstances. Indeed, many of the patterns of electronic play that have appeared in the twenty-first-century gaming world bear an uncanny resemblance to this kind of lost 'village' style of interaction, with groups of players forming tightly knit and intensely sociable online micro-communities, and undertaking often remarkably mundane in-game activities together simply for the pleasure of feeling that they truly belong within a particular (virtual) environment and to an intimate group of friends. Games, here, are not so much the cause of social pathologies as a refuge from them – and potentially a route out of them in a way that passively consumed media simply cannot be.

As the British author Naomi Alderman (who was living in Manhattan during and after 9/11) observed in an article for a British newspaper, video gaming offered her a vital refuge in the months after the attacks from a horrific reality she could do nothing to deal with or change. 'I remember surfacing from four-hour *Diablo II* sessions feeling as if I'd been on holiday, so grateful that I'd been able to blot out the images of genuine horror filling my city,' she wrote. 'The game was so mind-filling it left no room for the anxious brooding that I was experiencing the rest of the time. This was a tremendous blessing. For a few months, I played *Diablo II* for probably 30 hours a week, and I remain convinced that it was a pretty healthy response to the situation I was in. My desire to play the game faded as the city got back on its feet.'

In cultures like South Korea's, too, where playing games in

public internet cafés is the equivalent of going to a pub or bar in Britain or America, it's hard not to make the comparison between the booze-fuelled nightlife of a Western city and the buzz of one of Seoul's more than 10,000 'PC bangs', where the strongest stuff served tends to be coffee or energy drinks alongside a bowl of ramen noodles. There may be a lot of swearing and smoke in the air, but violence is almost unheard of, and gaming is considered an intensely sociable business (and a subject of great national pride). In South Korea, with entire television networks dedicated to broadcasting live matches of cult games such as *Starcraft*, pro-gamers are national celebrities and can earn hundreds of thousands of dollars a year. Gaming excellence, like sporting excellence, is seen as an aspiration, even a gift, and the games industry itself is increasingly being seen as a meeting place for some of the best and the brightest in the coming generation: a nexus of innovation and technical skills.

Perhaps above all, amid much of the media's insistent focus on certain negatives and dangers, it's important to maintain a sense of proportion – and of the ways in which gaming use so often defies every stereotype of both subject and attitude. Take my own entirely ordinary exploits within one of the most controversial games of all time, *Grand Theft Auto* IV, my pre-ordered copy of which joined the 608,999 other units sold in Britain on 29 April 2008. The game is full of pastiche violence, of slyly explicit dialogue and ceaseless minor homages to cinema, television and music. It has an 18 certificate, and I won't be inviting any nine-year-olds to join me in investigating its world. But the play experience is an open-ended delight of exploration around 'Liberty City', a lovingly detailed parallel New York, within which you can pass hours driving around in various vehicles, watching the sun rise and set, trying to attract the attention of cops and then shake them off, and – in one especially memorable moment – driving a stolen ambulance off a roadbridge on to a raised section of trainline, then manoeuvring it underground and through the 'Manhattan' railway network. All this is best done in company, and most of the pleasure I've taken from the game has involved sitting on a sofa with friends, dissecting the city and deriding each other's driving skills with gleeful abandon. It's quite a thing, too, to be moved by the beams of an unreal sun setting behind a not-quite-Manhattan skyline.

If you think this kind of reaction puts me on the outer fringe of unusual, think again. Most of the game's content and in-built achievements are geared around various kinds of exploration and driving tricks; the series' huge following is largely due not to its slick presentation or gangsta styling, but to the quality of the 'sandbox' it offers – that is, the non-linear, living and breathing tiny world it allows you to race anarchically around. This is where the root of its appeal lies: in something designed not simply to breed compulsion, but as an experiment with what it is that we find delightful, exciting, arresting and even beautiful. The common denominator here is far from what is widely assumed to be 'lowest' in human nature. Sex and violence, for instance, aren't nearly as high up the list of what most people demand from games as most critics assume. Of the twenty bestselling console games of all time, only one (a *Grand Theft*

Auto game, naturally enough) involves any real-world violence at all: the top slot is occupied by *Wii Play*, a family-friendly compendium of retro-pursuits like virtual fishing, laser hockey and billiards; No. 2, *Nintendogs*, is a 'pet' game that involves looking after and dressing up a cute pet dog; No. 3 is from the *Pokémon* series of cute role-playing games; and most of the others are driving or role-playing or platform games, all of which involve escape and vicarious thrills, but not violence in any pornographic sense. Similarly, the bestselling game series of all time is *The Sims*, a 'virtual life' simulation.

It's interesting to compare games, in this respect, to that other exponentially expanding technological phenomenon, the internet itself. During the first few years of the internet's existence, many serious commentators argued that it would inexorably become mired in pornography to the point where it could barely be used for anything else. Yet today, although pornography can indeed be accessed online in sufficient quantities to keep anyone who wants it supplied for the rest of their life, only a couple of the world's 100 most visited websites relate to pornography, and 99 per cent of web traffic is non-pornographic. Instead, people spend most of their time online on such activities as social networks, searching for news and other information, sharing (non-pornographic) images and videos, buying and selling goods and media – and, of course, in playing games, which is now the world's third largest internet-based activity after search and socialising.

All of which is to say that painting human nature as too violent and venal is itself a dangerous distortion in the struggle to understand our relationship with new media. It's a point that's made explicitly by one of the most significant documents yet to appear on society's relationship with the dangers and pleasures of this technology: Dr Tanya Byron's March 2008 review *Safer Children in a Digital World*, prepared at the request of the British government in an attempt to map out its digital strategy for Britain over the next decade. Commissioned in a climate of concerned headlines and parental unease, Byron's conclusions poured cold water on what could have been a conflagration of media hysteria. 'Having considered the evidence,' she wrote, 'I believe we need to move from a discussion about the media "causing" harm to one which focuses on children and young people, what they bring to technology and how we can use our understanding of how they develop to empower them to manage risks and make the digital world safer.' It may sound banal, but Byron's 226-page report is enormously valuable for the clarity of its assertion that the media debate must move on towards the adult business of education, contextualisation, responsible classification and regulation; and the early identification of those who may need support in their use of media, and indeed in their lives as a whole.

Finally, if there is one danger that is both real and often overlooked, it's the error of assuming that any medium can or should stand alone. It may be the apex of the uncontroversial to say that all human pursuits are diminished by excess – but the much-feared prospect that playing video games will automatically breed illiteracy, sloth and ignorance is not something that games themselves have any power to bring about. Balancing the multiplying demands of pleasure, leisure and work may be harder than ever in the twenty-first century, with more and more competing options for an often shrinking amount of free time. Understandably, there will always be those who wish to return to the alleged simplicities of an older world. But the present is in no way helped by the crude caricaturing of this youngest and most dynamic of our media; and the case cannot be made for the virtues of reading, conversation or even television-watching simply by pouring scorn on something else.

CHAPTER 6

The Warcraft effect

From the 1970s onwards, video games were increasingly being mentioned in novels, on television and in films. A fairly clear consensus soon emerged in these media about what games were and how they should be presented: they were esoteric creations, used exclusively by hollow-eyed adolescent males. These males were socially deficient. They probably had few friends, and the ones they did have were as sick as them. Game-playing adolescents were unhealthy, and would remain so until they kicked their electronic habit. Gaming, it seemed, was like an especially pernicious kind of masturbation: something that turned you in on yourself in the worst possible way. The 1993 film *Arcade* was a typical work along these lines, featuring a sinister video game in an arcade called, suspiciously, *Dante's Inferno*, with the ability to capture the souls and take over the minds of the lonely adolescents drawn to it. Hardly a subtle messge, but one that was often repeated.

This popular image was hugely unfair in many ways, but it

did have some elements of truth. For their first few decades, games were played largely by adolescent males. They did have a slightly cultish feel to them. And what gamers did, within either the lightless bowels of the video arcade or the closed-curtain fastness of the bedroom, was isolating in a larger social sense. This came about as the result of a combination of historical and technological coincidences. First, early games were primitive. Their manufacture was becoming increasingly less amateur, but they continued to look like what they were: an immature medium, unable to compete with the more fully realised arenas of film, print and music. Games were not fit for the living rooms or the polite conversations of the adult world: they appeared regressive, childish and antithetical to the fully developed social beings that it was dearly hoped each monosyllabic pubescent youth would grow into.

Second, and equally importantly, the development of simple and effective networking technologies lagged decades behind the development of affordable home computers and video games systems. In their early existence, therefore, most games could only have one or, at an occasional best, two players. Setting up and playing across a local area network or even just a serial connection between two computers was a mission certain to defeat all but the most dedicated gamers; and the two-player experiences that were available on consoles and in arcades remained fairly crude, and well within the accepted boundaries of 'cultish'.

Within the last decade, most of this has changed almost beyond measure, thanks to the combined influences of the internet and the increasing arrival of video gaming as a mainstream – and even a family-friendly – media activity. Yet many of the most fundamental questions about games' relationships with society and sociability haven't gone away. Today, books and films can't get away with crudely caricaturing games as adolescent curiosities; but nor does the emerging social culture of gaming have much in common with many of the older norms of civilised social interactions, or even traditional definitions of what it means to be sociable (which usually involves being in the same physical space as those people you're interacting with).

In a world where the internet already connects more than 1.5 billion people, and will in 2020 connect double that number, a whole new notion of sociability is being born and tested online. Yet this development has video games very close to its heart. It's easy to forget that the very idea of social networking, from Facebook to MySpace to Bebo or even Twitter, was pioneered by video games long before there was even such a thing as the internet – in the text-based multiplayer games of the 1970s and 1980s, and then in the online multiplayer games of the late 1990s. No other online social arena is so demanding, engaged, engrossing, immersive or sophisticated as gaming. And no other online activity, including social networking, is more popular between friends than the playing of video games.

Perhaps the most fundamental question of all here is how someone can be said to have 'met', let alone got to know or formed a friendship with, someone else when their relationship is entirely mediated through a screen. It's a question that mystifies and concerns many people of the non-gaming generation, and that even among gamers largely lacks any fixed points of reference or means of critical evaluation. But it's also an increasingly common, albeit implicit, assumption that the various virtual interactions in someone's life – their emails, their electronic chats and texts, their phone calls, their blog posts and shared photographs, their Amazon wish list and *Second Life* avatar – are collectively at least as revealing of who they are as the conversations they have with colleagues across a desk or with friends across a restaurant table. The very notion of what social interaction means is shifting fundamentally.

According to one influential and wide-ranging study, the 2008 Pew Internet/MacArthur Report on Teens, Video Games and Civics in the US, the great majority of game-playing today is a shared experience of some kind. Surveying over 1,000 teenagers, the group of players whose behaviour is probably the best indicator of larger trends to come, the Pew Internet/MacArthur report said that 94 per cent of American teenage girls played video games, as did 99 per cent of teenage boys; and that, across both sexes, 76 per cent reported that they played with friends, either in person or online. These numbers have steadily increased over the last decade – similar surveys in 2001 and 2003 put the figure at just over 60 per cent – and, given that all the most rapidly growing sectors of the industry today are linked in some way to social gaming, are certain to keep growing.

The trend is predictable enough in that, like sports, the pleasures of most games are best sampled in company. Each game is a live, unfolding performance to which every player brings something slightly different – and during which the pleasures of discovery, skill and achievement are invariably enhanced by the presence of a sympathetic audience. This is especially true of the genre of games designed to be played by friends or family members gathered in a living room: various party games on the Nintendo Wii, or performance games like *Guitar Hero* and *Rock Band* where much of the joy is – as with board games or watching live sports – in the atmosphere of the room itself, rather than anything in particular that's happening on the screen.

Still, perhaps the weightiest criticism of the impact of modern games derives from one fundamental point: that, in the majority of cases, the primary interaction is between a player and an unreal, onscreen realm. In contrast to unmediated face-to-face relations, the theory runs, these game-based interactions are inevitably diminished, and in turn diminish the things that flow from them, such as friendship, trust, commitment and affection. It's an argument that has been put eloquently by, among others, the philosopher Roger Scruton, whose position, as articulated in a 2008 article for *The Times*, is as follows:

In real life, friendship involves risk. The reward is great: help in times of need, joy in times of celebration. But the cost is also great: self-sacrifice, accountability, the risk of embarrassment and anger, and the effort of winning another's trust. Hence I can become friends with you only by seeking your company. I must attend to your words, gestures and body language, and win the trust of the person revealed in them, and this is risky business. I can avoid the risk and still obtain pleasure; but I will never obtain friendship or love.

When I relate to you through the screen there is a marked shift in emphasis. Now I have my finger on the button. At any moment I can turn you off ... Of course I may stay glued to the screen. Nevertheless, it is a screen that I am glued to, not the person behind it.

Scruton's critique is compelling in many ways and can, to some degree, be applied as a salutary warning to all forms of mediation between people. There is no substitute, he is arguing, for face-to-face contact in the development of a healthy mind and a fully developed social and moral life. This is difficult to disagree with. What he also seems to be implying is that modern technology encourages people to spend too much time interacting with each other remotely, and not enough time getting out of their homes or offices and taking the 'risk' of meeting in person. Again, it's difficult to disagree, in terms both of observable health and what people themselves say about their lives. 'Balance' is a difficult thing to achieve, and in everything from diet to health to family time, almost every society lags behind the ideal.

Should we then simply put up our hands and set about trying to minimise the quantity of these low-quality, remote interactions? Not quite. Scruton is making a general point about online culture rather than a specific one about video games. But at the root of his claim lies the assertion that it is 'a screen that I am glued to, not the person behind it'. And this is something that, when it comes to video games, fails to ring true in several crucial respects. Many gamers will, for instance, find it difficult to reconcile their social experiences within online games with the idea of something that's either 'risk-free' or regressive. A computer can of course be switched off at any time, just as a telephone can be slammed down or a letter ignored. But a game is a very different proposition to a simple conversation or an exchange of views, and its most fundamental appeal is something far more closely related to a player's abiding interest in the hazy workings of other people than their subservience to any implacable machine logic.

World of Warcraft – or *WoW*, as it's invariably known – is the world's most famous MMO. It's fascinating for many reasons, but perhaps the single most compelling one is its sheer success. At the time of writing, *WoW* boasted a still-rising total of over 12 million monthly subscribers, and annual revenues of well over $1 billion. Its sprawling, cartoonish fantasy world offers literally thousands of hours of content in the form of levelling up a character (or characters) by gaining experience points, exploring hundreds of varied and distinctively beautiful landscapes, undertaking quests in search of better equipment, and so on. Beyond all this, though, playing *WoW* soon opens any new players' eyes to a social experience whose richness, strangeness and layered possibilities constitute a more compelling reason for play than even the most expertly designed levels, items or reward sequences.

The sheer size and friendliness of the *WoW* community is a large part of this: the game has deliberately made itself accessible to 'non-hardcore' players and, crucially, allows people to show their full personalities and behaviour they are comfortable with, rather than expecting them to take the business of 'being' an orc or dwarf seriously. Players can do exactly that if they wish, on dedicated role-playing servers packed with Gandalfs and Saurons, but on the whole the game offers an extremely sophisticated combination of pop cultural references, witty visuals, clear practical explanations of what your options are, and plenty of opportunities for casual cooperation, bantering, learning and self-expression. Perhaps the single most popular character customisation involves owning – for purely aesthetic and emotional reasons – a wide variety of cute pets.

Equally, once a player starts to get the hang of the whole notion of playing and advancing a character within *WoW*, they'll soon discover that the various different 'classes' it's possible to play (each with their own specialised talents and limitations: a warrior is peerless in hand-to-hand combat, but lacks magic, healing abilities or projectile attacks; a mage is physically fragile, but able to wield various elemental abilities to do huge damage from a distance; a druid can transform into a variety of specialised animal incarnations, and so on) interlock in a progressively more complex set of permutations. It culminates, in the so-called 'end game', with parties of twenty-five or forty seasoned adventurers fighting their way through challenges that only the most precisely coordinated strategies and finely honed skills can beat. This demand for extremely sophisticated patterns of player behaviour and strategy creates a social environment that is in many ways more akin to a busy, ambitious office than a teenage slacker's lounge: one full of organisational necessities, political manoeuvrings and complex patterns of inter-reliance.

Adam Brouwer, in the guise of a ferocious orc warrior called Mogwai, started playing WoW the month it launched, in November 2004. A civil servant specialising in crisis modelling at work, he hurled himself into WoW with a ruthless panache honed by decades of gaming at home on everything from a primitive Amstrad computer to Sony's finest console offerings. First, there came the rush simply to explore and to progress: finding out what this virtual world had to offer, and trying to reach the 'level cap' beyond which a character cannot continue to increase their vital statistics. Then came the serious business of leaving his mark on the world.

As Adam soon discovered, the best way to combine pleasure and progress was to formally ally himself to other players within the structure of a guild. The medieval ring of this word is no coincidence. Guilds in the game are essentially feudal structures, consisting of a pyramid of autocratic power descending from a single leader through officers and members to the rank-and-file of wannabes and applicants. Anything from five to 500 players can be in the same guild, and their individual cultures are as varied as the people who play them. Often, real-life friends will create a loose, casual guild of mutual convenience to help them hook up online and join together in taking on a few big challenges. Meanwhile, bloodthirsty specialists in slaughtering other players might form a guild dedicated entirely to 'player versus player' mayhem. And truly ambitious players will vie to operate the most successful guild on a server, or even in the world, running their affairs according to fanatically strict operational timetables, membership rules, and even private monetary subscriptions from individual members.

For Adam, after a couple of years of membership in a variety of increasingly ambitious guilds dedicated to completing the game's very toughest challenges (for example, involving raiding parties of up to forty expert players), the moment eventually arrived when a power vacuum left him free to make a move for supreme authority. With the support of a few fellow players and a detailed strategic proposal, Adam became leader of a guild known as Adelante and promptly set about remoulding it in his own image. In May 2008, he was at his peak: 20,000 gold pieces in the bank, the two most powerful weapons in the game resting snugly on his back (the Twin Blades of Azzinoth, green-glowing monstrosities each the length of a full-grown orc), other players following him around just to glimpse the splendour that one day might be theirs. On the secondary market (an illegal but inexorable part of the *WoW* experience) he reckoned Mogwai might fetch up to $10,000. But he had no intention whatever of selling. For a start, having clocked up over 4,500 hours of play on this character alone, even an astronomical sum would hardly make it worth his while. More sentimentally, too, he felt this character was not his alone to sell. 'The strange thing about Mogwai is that he doesn't just belong to me,' he explained. 'Every item he has got through the hard work of twenty or more other people. Selling him would be a slap in their faces. When I started,

I didn't care about the other people. Now they are the only reason I continue.'

As Adam is acutely aware, the moment you start taking a more than entirely casual interest in a game like *WoW*, something paradoxical begins to happen. In a non-game online experience – browsing the internet or using any ordinary website – your relationship with the world onscreen is a largely casual one: you flick backwards and forwards, opening and closing windows at the click of a mouse. Far from this casualness being a modern ideal that people crave, however, it seems that they will go to quite extraordinary lengths to inject meaning into their online encounters: the entire phenomenon of guilds, complete with its connotations of cloistered medieval life, is ample testament to this, and is something that was developed over time entirely thanks to the efforts of players themselves rather than game designers. Gaming life is, in its way, thick with obligations, judgements and allegiances – and this is the way people like it. What they crave is not so much an escape from or avoidance of the commitments that make for 'real' friendships and worldly achievements as the opportunity to conjure virtual versions of the same class of satisfaction.

Take the activities of Adam/Mogwai and his fellow guild members during a typical 'raiding mission'. First, a team of twenty-five players with a carefully balanced spectrum of abilities and equipment must meet at a pre-arranged time and place, under an agreed leader. All players must remain in vocal communication, via microphones and headsets, at all times. The raid itself might take up to ten hours, and is to be conducted according to a painfully researched strategy. Essentially an assault on a heavily fortified dungeon, it will entail mass attacks on a succession of powerful computer-controlled 'boss' creatures, each with unique abilities, demanding a unique attack strategy. Players with missile abilities will attack from a distance, healers will keep other players alive, while melee specialists will engage at close quarters, all to a strict timetable. The rewards gained from each encounter – which usually take the form of rare and powerful weapons, armour and trinkets that can be used by in-game characters – will be allocated according to an in-guild system, depending upon rank, experience, need, contribution and the whim of the guild leader. Those failing to pull their weight could face being summarily ejected.

A raid is an extreme example, but this is the kind of complex, pressurised scenario that all games force on their players in some way, in which one lapse of concentration can – and frequently does – mean having to do things again, or losing. Tempers fray, and leadership qualities are severely tested. As Adam explained it, 'a successful guild leader needs to be thick-skinned, capable with the carrot and the stick, able to deal with a wide variety of people of different sexes, backgrounds, ages and egos'. And all the people within a guild, or simply playing alongside one another, need to be able to deal with each other: there are few environments more likely to bring the essential features of a personality to the fore than the intensely inter-reliant pressure-cooker of a game.

It's not just gamers who are noticing the significance and scale of this. Adam cited a recent article in the *Harvard Business*

Review, billed under the line 'The best sign that someone's qualified to run an internet startup may not be an MBA degree, but level 70 guild leader status'. In fact, the article argued, it was increasingly true that games allow people to learn new ways of thinking about leadership in a digital world that are far ahead of most practices in the world of business itself: 'Perhaps the most striking aspect of leadership in online games is the way in which leaders naturally switch roles, directing others one minute and taking orders the next. Put another way, leadership in games is a task, not an identity – a state that a player enters and exits rather than a personal trait that emerges and thereafter defines the individual.'

If you used that argument within the traditional business market you would, Adam felt, probably still 'get laughed out of the interview'. But things are changing fast, and he already counts himself among those whose real-life career and skills have benefited significantly from their gaming activities. 'In *Warcraft* I've developed confidence; a lack of fear about entering difficult situations; I've enhanced my presentation skills and debating. Then there are more subtle things: judging people's intentions from conversations, learning to tell people what they want to hear. I am certainly more manipulative, more Machiavellian. I love being in charge of a group of people, leading them to succeed in a task.'

It's an observation that chimes with the feelings of many other gamers in a similar position, some of whom don't share Adam's reservations about the attitude of the traditional business market towards gaming as an indicator of certain skills. Guild leader

Craig McKechnie has, for instance, been playing games since he was a child, and even spent a stint on the American pro-gaming circuit during his late teens. Craig has headed several successful guilds, first in *Ultima Online* and then, perhaps inevitably, in *WoW*, and now lives in Massachusetts with two people he met via online games. He also works for a major bank, and feels no obligation to conceal his love of gaming from his employers. 'When I was hired,' he explains, 'I was asked why I left running my guild off my résumé. A Vice President of the company told me that it shows great leadership and responsibility, and not to leave it off future applications.'

Although it still has a ring of novelty to it, Craig's observation invokes an attitude that has long prevailed in the world of business: the right kind of play can be both profoundly revealing and motivating. A round of golf can reveal more about a CEO than a hundred more formal meetings. Team games can produce more bonding and mutual understanding than any amount of time spent sharing an office. The problem is not so much injecting meaning into gaming interactions: it's coping with the level of commitment, energy and self-articulation that they demand.

In June 2009, Adam faced one of the biggest watersheds of his gaming life: his decision to step down as guild leader and cease playing *World of Warcraft*. Five years after he first logged on, and with over 6,000 hours invested in the character of Mogwai, a combination of factors had, he explained, meant that he now felt his time playing *WoW* should end. What was going on? 'I felt a sense of disillusionment with where the game was going.

Key guild players were moving on themselves. And, probably more vitally, I've had a realignment of my own priorities.' This, he swiftly added, no more represented a disillusionment with video games as a whole than stopping watching a particular drama series might spell a disillusionment with television. 'It really culminated with me realising I wanted to play other games, games with a pause button.'

In Richard Bartle's terms, Adam had reached the end of his heroic journey, at least within WoW. One thing that was especially striking about this process, however, was just how elaborate a procedure it was for him to exit the guild and the game. Couldn't he, in Scruton's terms, simply decide one day to hit the off button and never show his virtual face in WoW again? 'Oh God, no. You don't just leave over thirty-five people in the lurch like that, especially not from a position of authority. I pretty much made the decision four months ago. Then I gave warning to the officer corps that my interest in the game was waning. I selected the new leadership, and made sure the guild would keep going without me; then I gradually weaned myself off it, raiding less frequently, leading less from the front.' It all sounds rather better planned than many corporate exit strategies, which perhaps shouldn't come as a surprise given the formality of the processes involved in joining and putting together a guild like Adam's in the first place: written applications, in-depth interviews, probationary periods.

Still, there were inevitably mixed feelings as he mulled over his time in the game. 'It was fulfilling to commit to something and actually to reach and perhaps surpass my own expectations.

At the same time, you realise it's not something that you can really take with you. Friendships were lost as well as made. I was very guilty of taking it far too seriously.' Yet, as Adam himself added, one thing he could take away was the friendships and, in all its odd complexities, the human experience of the game. In fact, he added, what he was hoping for in leaving was to escape from an excessively sociable experience: 'Dealing with different personality types, getting them to do things, handling the constant turnover. It had its benefits, like being able to indulge an aspect of myself that wouldn't be acceptable in a normal work environment. But after a while it can all get too much.'

When considering just how 'real' anything that can be taken away from a video game is, it's also worth taking into account the degree to which most real-life activities, from work to shopping to dating, demand a degree of self-concealment precisely because they carry the possibility of real-life consequences. Video games, in this sense, are not so much more (or less) real behavioural environments than they are different ones, with their own particular kind of authenticity on offer.

One thing that almost all academics can agree about is that the strange mix of freedom and constraint found within games has a magnifying effect on personalities. Those with altruistic and team-building inclinations express them more strongly, as do those with anarchistic and abusive tendencies. People are freer to act within a virtual environment in several senses: there is a freedom from major consequences of their actions, but also a freedom to put their time and resources at others' disposal. The banter can be brutal, but conversations can also cut through to the essentials almost at once. Perhaps most significantly of all, a virtual world is also a tremendous leveller in terms of wealth, age, appearance and race. It's a place where 'you' are entirely composed of your words and actions, and for anyone who isn't in the optimum social category of, say, being attractive and aged between twenty and thirty-five, the benefits of being able simply to circumvent any kind of prejudice are potentially huge.

This notion of equality is something that's of central interest to Ville and Liz Lehtonen, a husband and wife who have between them devoted a large proportion of the last decade to various kinds of video game. When Ville first met Liz (or, if you prefer, first 'met' Liz: this was a strictly virtual encounter), he was living in Finland and she was living in the western United States. Their game of choice was *EverQuest*, a sword-and-sorcery style MMO run by Sony since 1999; and Ville was the co-leader of a guild Liz had joined. He had been away for three months and, as she puts it, 'when he came back he was so bossy and annoying and irrational that I wrote him an email saying all this. He wrote back having a go at me. We talked, and he thought I was cute, and it went from there. We met up in Paris about 3 or 4 months later; and I ended up moving to Finland.'

It's a whirlwind romance, on paper, and yet, by their reckoning, Liz and Ville must have spent several hundred hours in conversation before their first face-to-face meeting. And it's this that was the key to the success of their relationship. As Liz explained, 'I find that I have a tendency to be more open with people that I meet online. It's easier to be much more negative too, but I think you're quite a bit closer to the people who you do really like.' It's a view that Ville seconds. 'For me, real relationships had often tended to be more superficial. In real life it takes a lot more for people to express their true feelings. Whereas, if people like you online, that to me is much more certain than with people in real life, who might just like the way you look or find you convenient because you are useful to them rather than genuinely wanting your company.'

In one sense, it's possible to think about online games as a kind of highly sophisticated dating site. By his own estimate, Ville spoke to between 50 and 200 people a day as the leader of a major *EverQuest* guild and the game was crucial in making these interactions more than casual. In providing context, focus and circumstances, people soon revealed some fairly significant information about just how well they could work in a team, take constructive criticism, express their intentions verbally, and generally manage to relate to a diverse bunch of people.

Perhaps more surprisingly, though, Ville also discovered a community profoundly interested in certain fundamental political and philosophical principles: notions of fairness, of co-operation, of justice and of competition. One example, he explains, is the great *EverQuest* debate about 'Communism versus Capitalism', that is, an argument between players as to how the limited resources available within the game should be divided between those paying to play it. The problem itself seems simple. Each game server in *EverQuest* can have around 5,000 people playing on it at one time, all of whom will be paying an identical amount of money – $10, give or take – to Sony each month for the privilege. In order to make the game worth playing there are naturally strictly limited numbers of the most dangerous enemies in the game, enemies who, if players can manage to kill them, are likely to yield up some of the most powerful items it's possible to own. So, for example, there may be only fifty rare blue dragons available for potential slaughter during the course of any given month.

Unlike *World of Warcraft*, *EverQuest* has no closed dungeons within which a group of players can 'raid' undisturbed: everything is out in the open and up for grabs. So, while a 'fair' division of these fifty blue dragons between the 5,000 people on a server would mean that 100 or so people would be allowed to have a go at teaming up and killing each dragon, in practice the same elite guild ends up killing almost every single dragon due to its superior skills, dedication, contacts and resources. Sony and *EverQuest* allow this: it's not against the rules, or even against the spirit, of the game. The result, however, is a quite stupendous level of debate in both the game itself and the huge number of player-run forums, websites and discussion boards surrounding it: who is entitled to what; can a consensual system be arrived at to ensure the fair division of virtual goods between all players; what obligations do players have to each other, or the game's designers to their players?

This arena of often fantastically detailed discourse is known as the 'meta-game', and its influence extends well beyond private squabbles, grudges and flames. Visit any website devoted to hosting player discussions of games like *World of Warcraft*, for instance, and you'll find not hundreds but tens of thousands of comments flying between players who debate every aspect of the game, from weapon-hit percentages to detailed mathematical analyses of the most efficient sequence in which to use a character's abilities. It will range from the sublime to the ridiculous, and will invariably be riddled with private codes, slang, trolls, flames, and everything else the internet so excels at delivering. What you'll find above all, though, is a love of discussion almost for its own sake; and an immensely broad and well-informed range of critical analyses. It's not uncommon for doctors or professors of economics or maths to wade into the fray – and find themselves bested by other still more meticulous chains of gamer reasoning. Doctoral theses can and have been spun out of MMO forums. It's a richness that flows in both directions between the game worlds themselves and the sprawling social arenas that surround them.

Perhaps the most sophisticated MMO of them all, the epic science fiction universe EVE *Online*, has even seen its player community persuade the company running the game to hold democratic elections for a 'council' via which players can voice their concerns directly to developers. Places on this Council of Stellar Management, as it's known, were first competed for in a full election during March 2008, with sixty-six candidates putting themselves forward for nine positions. Every player of the game was eligible to vote, and the results were announced in May 2008: 24,651 votes were cast out of a pool of 222,422 eligible voters, revealing a turnout of 11.08 per cent – not bad at all, considering the level of engagement with the game required to follow the campaigning and select between the candidates –

with victories for some of the most well-known and vocal members of the player community. These days, alongside the Council, there is also a separate Internal Affairs division, designed to root out misconduct on the part of both players and developers after some nasty allegations of 'insider dealing' with valuable engineering schematics. It's a grand experiment in community government and participation that is only just beginning, but has staggering potential, given the sheer number and diversity of players involved in online games like EVE.

All of this is also extremely significant in terms what 'anti-social' actually means. Video games, it often seems, can be companionable to play, but tend to go hand-in-hand with a larger social disengagement, substituting a diffuse non-local network of contacts for immediate relationships with a local community or even country. It's certainly true that internet sub-culture has always had a somewhat libertarian bent to it, with avid gamers tending to be less religious, less dogmatic and less locally minded than national populations as a whole.

As a tool for broadening people's perspectives, this is often a very good thing. Even casual gamers like my wife and myself have developed dozens of good in-game friendships with people from, for example, small towns in the southern and central US that we would never have visited or learned anything about in a hundred years of non-virtual travel. Yet these are now places we have visited on several occasions, just as these friends have visited us, broadening both sets of horizons in the process. It's easy to see, however, how the very ease of establishing such transnational relations might undermine one's loyalty and commitment to a genuinely local community, not to mention to the necessary trappings of government and civil society – voting, taxation, looking out for one's neighbours, using and investing in local facilities, even something as simple as keeping a house and garden tidy.

Many gamers will simply sniff at such observations. For national governments and societies, however, there is potentially a large problem here. How can a nation command loyalty – and rely on the participation of its citizens in everything from voting to paying taxes to keeping their front gardens tidy – in a world where people are increasingly free to chose their own loyalties irrespective of where they happen to be living?

Video games are an especially interesting medium in this respect, because both the problem and the solution may be two sides of the same coin. If you really want people to participate in twenty-first-century democracy, the kind of behaviours and institutions that have developed within online games are pretty hard to beat as motivating, co-operative social tools. Unlike any other form of online activity, or indeed any other medium or recreation, games have already got it all: elections, formal debates and fundamental discussions, self-organising task-forces, mass communications and mass motivations, human groupings which largely transcend age, gender, sex, physique and wealth.

On top of this, one of the most unexpected results of the 2008 Pew Internet & American Life Project was the degree to which gaming communities already seemed to be unusually aware of current social and political issues, and more likely than the population as a whole to take political action. More than half the gamers surveyed reported that games 'made them think about moral and ethical issues', while 43 per cent reported that games involved making 'decisions about how a community, city or nation should be run', and 40 per cent reported that playing games had taught them about a particular social issue.

The degree to which online communities can feed directly into politics was powerfully illustrated in 2009 via an unorthodox Swedish political movement called the Pirate Party. Effectively the political wing of the file-sharing website The Pirate Bay, the Pirate Party campaigned for radical changes in copyright and patent laws as well as a greater right to privacy for individuals. So far, so dull: the Party had been born at the start of 2006, and done relatively little beyond publish manifestos during the first few years of its life. Things changed, however, in April 2009, when the founders of the Pirate Bay website were found guilty of copyright infringement. Within hours of the verdict, membership of the Pirate Party began to soar. Within a week, it had more members than all but three of the parties in the Swedish government. Then, still more surprisingly, in the 2009 European parliamentary elections it managed to win no less than 7.13 per cent of the national vote, entitling it to a seat in the European Parliament.

File-sharing and gaming communities are very different. But to those 'digital natives' in their early teens embarking now into the online world, the barriers between friendships, play, cultural discourse and everyday communications are increasingly not so much permeable as non-existent. With online 'counter-culture' fast approaching the point where it has a similar number of active participants to the mainstream culture it is supposed to be against, it's time to realise that games represent a substantial social force that needs to be plugged into the mainstream of cultural and political life as rapidly as possible. Politicians and businessmen hoping to thrive in the digital world would do better to study games for tips on everything from leadership to community organisation than to waste their time discussing the vanished dream of an unmediated society.

Chapter 7

Clouds and flowers

In December 1895, the Lumière brothers, Auguste and Louis, showed the first films of real-life images to a paying audience, in Paris. In jerking black and white, people watched workers leaving a factory, bathers splashing around in the sea and – most famously – a train rushing into a station, the sight of which sent many spectators running out of the room in terror. It sounds banal today, yet such was the novelty and astonishing power of the moving image that many people simply could not believe it was being generated by a machine.

Here was a medium, but not yet an art form – much as, several thousand years earlier, the earliest known forms of writing had emerged not as a means of self-expression, but as a simple accounting method for tallying Mesopotamian crops and taxes. Film, too, for its first decade, was largely a novelty, a technological wonder whose purpose was simply to amaze – and turn a profit. From around the turn of the century, film increasingly became a medium of public entertainment as well as mere spectacle; but the notion of multi-reel 'feature films' did not become widespread until the time of the First World War, some twenty-five years after the moving picture's début. The advent of sound, in 1928, was another watershed for the medium, but although great cinematic works were now being produced, it took several decades more for film to master its own, unique artistic language: cinematography. It took time, too, for audiences to expect more from it than raw wonder or exhilaration; yet today it would be difficult to find a single person who does not admire at least one film as a work of art.

When it comes to video games, however, any enquiry will soon turn up people who've never even played them, let alone consider them of any artistic interest. This is hardly surprising. Commercial games have been around for less than four decades and, at first glance, it can seem that most of them remain, in artistic terms, at the level of cinema's train entering a station – occasions for technological shock and awe rather than for the more densely refined emotions of art.

Yet the nature of games as a creative medium has changed profoundly in recent years; and, increasingly, it's become difficult to draw any firm dividing line between many of the creative processes that go into making a successful game, and those that go into creating a film, or even a work of literary fiction or two-dimensional art. Take the case of Justin Villiers, an award-winning screenwriter and film-maker who since late 2007 has been plying his trade in the realm of video games. A decade ago, his career move would have been unthinkable for anyone serious about the artistic values of the medium they were working in.

Today, though, he believes that distinction has almost entirely vanished. 'In the old days the games industry fed on itself. You'd have designers who were brought up on video games and tired genre movies writing games themselves, so they were entirely self-referential; all the characters sounded like refugees from weak *Star Trek* episodes or *Lord of the Rings* out-takes. But now, there is new blood in the industry: not just in the writing, but in the whole creative process; people with backgrounds in cinema and theatre and comic books and television.'

It's a process that has, if anything, been accelerating with each passing year: the quality of writing attracts A-list actors, the financial success of games and the shifting demographic of their audience draws in leading directors and composers and even authors. Indeed, the sheer speed of this transition is now one of the defining artistic facts about the medium. Every year, Villiers explains, 'a new game will appear that wows us with something never seen before: a narrative design, a game play technique, a hardware coup. It's an industry growing fast but not remotely close to being fully realised. In the area in which I work, writing and direction, games are just starting to offer real catharsis, or to bring about epiphanies; they're becoming more than simply tools to sublimate our desires or our fight for survival.'

In terms of the analogy with film, he continues, 'it reminds me of the late 1960s and early 1970s in film-making, because there were no rules, or, as soon as there were some, someone would come along and break them. Kubrick needed a lens for *2001: a Space Odyssey* that didn't exist, so, together with the director of photography, he invented one. For *The Shining*, he wanted the camera to move in a certain way, so he invented the steady cam. It's like that in the industry right now. Around a table you have the creative director, lead animator, game designer, sound designer and me, and we're all trying to work out how to create a moment in a game or a sequence that has never been done before, ever. We're literally having to invent new methods and technology to realise our dreams.'

The issue of compromise is also not as fraught as might be expected, given the demands of writing for an interactive medium. 'Where there's money there is of course compromise,' Villiers explains. 'But, if anything, there is more freedom in game development. Television and film have settled into tired, sellable genres being made by people desperate to keep their jobs as advertising revenues fall and people consume other media. Games are still in a position to startle and surprise.' This ability to experiment is one of the most significant artistic assets gaming has. It is, now, a very big business indeed, yet the idealism and energy of the bright young people flocking towards it is a powerful counterbalance to the deadening hand of commercial realities. Where bestselling books and top-grossing films are often formulaic, the games charts are consistently packed with clever, innovative, paradigm-busting titles whose production standards – and whose close relationship with a critically engaged audience – are second to none.

Exactly how artistically sophisticated the process of creating a modern game is can only really be appreciated by looking at the process in detail. With over 220 employees, Blitz Games Studios is one of the largest independent makers of video games in Britain – and a fine place to follow the intricacies of turning a major game from a concept into a playable reality. It's a process that, as Blitz's senior concept artist Bob Cheshire knows better than most, demands much more than mere keyboard and mouse crunching. 'Drawing and painting, these are the most important things for anyone wanting to do my job. Plus the ability to turn over ideas fast and to create a world from scratch, visually. You have to be able to conjure up everything from brands and logos to products, furniture and streets.' A typical mainstream game involves producing many hundreds of hand-made images before any computer is even touched: drawings that provide the conceptual context – and inspiration – for the teams of other artists who will bring every detail of a new world to life.

After the concept art, a game's dedicated three-dimensional art team step in to turn these sketches first into detailed schematic drawings, then into 3D models composed from polygons. Again, traditional art skills top the list of requirements for anyone in this sector: the ability not only to sketch by hand, but also to model in clay, and to understand the contours and musculatures of both people and objects. Even when a three-dimensional world exists, however, less than half the artistic battle is complete. Now life and motion need to be conjured, another set of skills rooted in long-established artistic principles rather than hard science. The key textbook for young animators teaches the same 12-point method that Walt Disney's studio established in the 1930s. Momentum and the illusion of weight can make all the difference between something that appears to possess real life and something that merely moves – and, given that every object within a game is by definition mere weightless pixels, it can only be produced by careful artistry.

Then comes the sound. Unlike a film or television programme, a game begins entirely silent: every sound in it must, like every graphical pixel, be conjured from scratch, via a combination of location, studio and stock work, not to mention voice recording and music. This includes the entire business of scripting and directing what may be up to 100 hours or more of in-game scenes and interactions; complete with, increasingly, motion-capture techniques pioneered by the film industry that transfer real actors' performances almost directly onto computer-generated characters. There's no chance of drumming up a coach-load of extras for crowd scenes, of course: everything you see in a game will have followed the same labour-intensive path of concept art, 3D modelling, surface texturing, animation and the addition of sound.

It's only after all this creation has taken place that a game is actually slotted together into a coherent whole, integrated with its rules, layouts, interface, control systems, rewards, structure and dynamics. After all this, the studio then faces a mammoth series of quality control milestones to be passed, with testers putting in hundreds and even thousands of hours to ensure that every element of the game functions as it should. In a virtual world, nothing can be taken for granted; there is no reality beyond the fiction the game itself generates, and this must be maintained at all costs.

Much of this process is remarkably similar to the engineering behind some of the most critically acclaimed – and commercially successful – films of recent times, those produced using computer animation by Pixar Studios. From its first feature film, *Toy Story*, in 1995 to its tenth and most recent, *Up*, in 2009, Pixar has set a new standard for world-building that is in many ways impossible to distinguish from the processes described above at Blitz. From concept art to three-dimensional animation, the skills involved are identical and, given the ever-increasing power of computers, there's every reason to suppose that games every bit as stunning as Pixar films will be appearing before too long (in fact, the best modern games are already coming pretty close to *Toy Story*).

Graphics, though, aren't primarily what make Pixar films – or indeed any films – great. Their claim as art rests on a combination of plotting, characterisation and great cinematographic skill, and it's here that the discussion begins to get interesting. Although games can borrow much from other media, it's in their own unique qualities that their most significant artistic claims really stand or fall. The most important single factor here is interactivity: the constant feedback between user and game that sets games entirely apart from other media, and that brings with it a set of urgent aesthetic questions. If video games are art, what kind of art are they? What is unique and particular to them? And, perhaps most important, just how great is their potential?

Rhianna Pratchett, daughter of the bestselling fantasy fiction author Terry Pratchett and herself the lead writer for some of the most critically and commercially successful console titles of recent years, is someone to whom these ideas are familiar. Her father, the creator over more than twenty-five years of one of the most richly imagined and wittiest fantasy worlds in literary history, the Discworld, was heavily involved in 1995 with what proved to be the first of four adaptations of the Discworld into a video game. Terry Pratchett is also, as he's noted several times in interviews, an avid PC gamer who believes in taking the medium seriously, and who can boast the rare distinction of having given in 2008 a live interview entirely from within *Second Life* (when, asked whether *Second Life* would appear in any of his books, he replied, 'As far as I am concerned, my books are *Second Life*'). For Rhianna, though, it's an equation that operates precisely the other way around: the games are the primary medium of expression, with journalism and other writing very much a secondary concern. Consequently, her perception of games' artistic capabilities and their limitations is an acute one. 'They're not always good art and they occupy a different definition of "art" than we've previously been used to. They embody the art of the journey: interactivity, exploration, adventure – a kind of high-octane theatre with a shattered fourth wall.' And their limitations? 'Aesthetically speaking, there are some incredibly beautiful works of art in the video game world. However, I think there's certainly a lot of scope to improve the emotional and narrative depth in games and create deeper and more immersive stories and characters.'

Games, she believes, are a medium in which both writers and artists can scale similar heights to those they have achieved in other media in the past – but only if they're able to embrace the differences of the new form. 'I really enjoyed the way in which

Bioshock used environmental storytelling to underlie its core narrative,' she tells me, invoking one of the most praised games of 2007 and a title that's still an industry benchmark for its architecture (it's set in a parallel world in the year 1960 within a submarine art-deco-inspired dystopia that one's of the most memorable unreal places it's ever been possible for a gamer to visit). Similarly, the work she's most proud of doing herself is more of an achievement in incremental world-building than a single flash of inspiration: 'I think my work on the *Overlord* series has probably been my proudest achievement as a whole. This now encompasses four and a half games (*Overlord, Overlord: Raising Hell, Overlord II, Overlord: Dark Legend* and *Overlord: Minions*). I've established a great working relationship with the developers (Triumph Studios and Climax) as well as the publisher behind the titles (Codemasters.) As well as writing the scripts, co-designing the stories and directing the audio on the titles, I was also involved in the marketing and PR behind them. It's allowed me to give the series a very consistent voice, which so few writers get the chance to do in this industry.'

Players in a well-made game relish not only its appearance and its immediate thrills, but their experience of it as a conceptual and even an architectural space: something to be inhabited and savoured in its details, whether these are niceties of script or more abstract features of level design. Another favourite game, Rhianna notes, is the exploration-intensive 2005 game *Psychonauts*, which 'took level design as story to a whole new plateau, while managing to be both funny and emotionally moving at the same time'. The artistry here is almost a collaborative process between a game's creators and the player, whose explorations bring surprise, delight, learning and gradual mastery within a space that is finely balanced between freedom and constraint. It is an experience, at its best, pitched somewhere between walking into a story and swinging through a playground. And it is something that remains barely in its infancy as far as future potential is concerned.

One man pushing hard against existing conceptions of what it means to experience a game artistically is Jenova Chen, the co-founder and creative director of California-based games studio thatgamecompany. Chen's is a young firm whose mission, as he sees it, is breathtakingly simple: to produce games that are 'beneficial and relevant to adult life; that can touch you as books, films and music can'. Now in his late twenties, Chen was born and raised in Shanghai, where he played computer games and learned to program from the age of eight. He still remembers the first time a game truly affected him: when, at the age of thirteen, he played a famous Chinese adventure game called *The Legend of Sword and Fairy*. It is, he told me, 'a game that has deeply affected a whole generation of Chinese. Its plot, especially the ending, has moved many players to tears; near the end of the game, one of the female lead characters sacrifices her life. As a kid who at the time was forbidden from watching any adult television or films, or from reading any mature novels, I had never experienced high-level literature or art. So this game was my very first encounter with a deep sense of loss and grief, and because of that very first moment it had a great impact on me.'

Chen went on to excel at both computing and visual arts at school before taking a degree in computing in China. Having graduated, like many of China's ablest students he applied for a master's degree in the United States. By chance, this was in 2003, just a year after the University of Southern California had started offering a new course in interactive media. They suggested Chen apply, which he did; and the result was something that, as he put it, changed his life. 'After I came to the US, the University of Southern California took all of us on the course to the 2004 Game Developers Conference in California. This was my first time, and I saw over 20,000 people from all around the world gathered together, sharing ideas about games and giving lectures. It was just a very, very vivid scene. There was a lot of positive energy. My parents had always said I could never make a career by playing games, and I had thought when I was in China that making games was somehow shameful, like making pornography. But seeing this industry and this conference and all these passionate people, I told myself that this was an industry worthy of respect, worthy of academic study. It was something that could bring my parents a sense of honour.'

Chen completed his studies, founded his company, and the rest is history. He has now made three commercial games – *Cloud, flOw* and *Flower* – and each has been driven above all by his belief in games as a medium worthy of pride and excellence. Each has also been, in its way, a reworking of the same central principle, that games are 'for' many more people than currently think of themselves as gamers, and that the great task of game development is to bring the gaming experience to those millions of people who believe that video games are a shallow, foolish waste of time, and not for them. Chen is out, in other words, to prove these people wrong in the best manner possible – by presenting them with games that will change the way they think. 'Outside the traditional games market,' he tells me, 'is a huge other market full of people ready to enjoy interactive experiences: but no one has been making them for these people. So the question is, how do you design a game so that it will allow both new and old gamers to enjoy it in their own ways?'

Part of the answer is also the title of Chen's second game, *flOw*, a name he took from the psychological theory of the same name. As Chen sees it, 'You have to find a way to make the game adaptive, so that different players can enjoy it in their own way. That is the thing about interactive media, that they have the power to read input from a player and then to adapt. The flow experience describes how a person engaged in an activity finds that their ability and the challenge have reached a state of balance, at which point they enter a state where they start to lose themselves in the process.' It's an idea more usually associated with performance and creation than artistic appreciation. For Chen, though, it embodies the possibility of a truly immersive game, one in which any player is transported effortlessly into a state where discovery and exploration aren't so much about a battle for mastery (as in the *Tetris* model of play) as about an open-ended, constant series of actions and responses. The intention is to lead players not towards victory or loss, but to allow these constant shifting signals and responses themselves to become an artistic experience.

Chen's latest game, *Flower*, is the first true fulfilment of these ambitions, a work whose genesis sounds closer to that of a poem or a painting than an interactive entertainment. 'I grew up in Shanghai, a huge city, one of the world's biggest and most polluted. Then I came to America and, one day, I was driving from Los Angeles to San Francisco, and I saw endless fields of green grass, and rows and rows of windmill farms. And I was shocked, because in the twenty-four years of life I had had up until then, I had never seen a scene like this. So I started to think about a game; and I thought, wouldn't it be nice to turn a console into a portal, so you could enter this virtual room that allows you to enjoy the endless green fields of nature.'

The development process was driven in its initial stages by an exploration of this feeling of wonder and escape into nature. 'We initially focused on the feeling of being completely surrounded and embraced by nature: every individual blade of grass, the details on every flower. I was very interested in combining flowers with green fields of grass, to create a kind of exaggerated, crafted version of my impressions of nature. But then, after we accomplished this in virtual space, I started to feel there was something missing. Spending five or ten minutes in this space was awesome, but after this you felt something vital missing; it started to feel lonely, unsafe, strange, because there was nothing human in your sight. So I started to do concept art, these views of flowers with a little house or city added in the distance; and eventually, the game evolved into this love-letter towards both nature and the urban life, and trying to reach a harmony between the two.'

123

The actual experience of playing *Flower* is at once incredibly simple and compelling. Players control a petal from a single flower, and must move it around a shimmering landscape of fields and a gradually approaching city by directing a wind to blow it along, gathering other petals from other flowers as they go. Touch a button on the control pad to make the wind blow harder; let go to soften it; gently shift the controller in the air to change directions. You can, as I did on my first turn, simply trace eddies in the air, or gust between tens of thousands of blades of grass. Or you can press further into the world of the game and begin to learn how the landscape of both city and fields is altered by your touch, springing into light and life as you pass.

'We want the player to feel like they are healing,' Chen says, 'that they are creating life and energy and spreading light and love.' If this sounds hopelessly naive, it is important to remember that the sophistication of a game experience depends not so much on its conceptual complexity as on the intricacy of its execution. In *Flower*, immense effort has gone into making something that appears simple and beautiful but is minutely reactive and adaptable. Here, the sensation of flow – of immersion in the task of illumination and exploration – connects to some of those fundamental emotions that are the basis of all enduring art: its ability to enthral and transport its audience, to stir in them a heightened sense of time and place.

Still, an important question remains. What can't games do artistically? On the one hand, work such as Chen's points to a huge potential audience for whole new genres of game. On the other hand, there are certain limitations inherent in the very fabric of an interactive medium, perhaps the most important of which is also the most basic: its lack of inevitability. As the tech-savvy critic and author Steven Poole has argued in his book *Trigger Happy* (2000), 'great stories depend for their effect on irreversibility – and this is because life, too, is irreversible. The pity and terror that Aristotle says we feel as spectators to a tragedy are clearly dependent on our apprehension of circumstances that cannot be undone.' Games have only a limited, and often incidental, ability to convey such feelings, and this limitation reinforces an obvious point: that the invention of a new medium does not invalidate the need for or the value of older media. But it also raises the spectre of an important objection to games as a whole, that in their absorbing unreality, they somehow become less and less life-like as they create more and more engrossing alternative worlds; and that the kind of pleasure they offer is fundamentally one of escape rather than of engagement. As such, it might be felt that games cannot engage lastingly with many of the greatest and most enduring themes of art: the distinctly physical issues of violence, injustice, suffering, love, hatred; the creation of life and its ending.

Can games touch upon these themes profoundly? It seems reasonable to point out that death, injury, violence and suffering are not of course 'real' within any form of art – this being the point of art in the first place. In terms of form and constraint, moreover, a growing number of game designers motivated explicitly by 'artistic' intentions are beginning to challenge the point

Poole raises, that the lack of formal restrictions and irreversibility is a deficiency wired into their very being.

One such designer is Jason Rohrer, whose minimalistic game *Passage* is an explicit riposte to the argument that video games are unable to engage meaningfully with mortality. In some ways, *Passage* is even more akin to a poem than *Flower*. It's a game that always takes exactly five minutes to play, that occupies so little room that it fits into less disk space than a single medium-sized photographic image (less than 500kb), and that is controlled simply by using the arrow keys on a computer keyboard to move through a blocky, maze-like landscape that can only be seen as a narrow passage of visibility ahead and behind at the centre of an otherwise entirely blank screen. The graphics are approximately as sophisticated as those from a late-1980s computer game.

What, then, is its point? In one sense, the point is points: these appear at the top right corner of your narrow passage of visibility, and are gained by every step taken and by the sporadic discovery of treasure chests. The points, though, serve little good in the long run. Every game lasts exactly five minutes, with the character's position within *Passage*'s narrow landscape inexorably shifting from left to right across the screen no matter where he is moved within it, and then the game is over. A tiny grave suddenly appears, indicating that he has expired. Sometimes, if a particular route has been chosen, a player will have been joined for most of their journey by a female companion; but she always dies too, just before the player. After a few mystifying games, it becomes a curiously moving experience to play – exploring this narrow world as time ticks away, watching the darkness creeping towards your character, gathering points or simply strolling beside a companion as the identical end approaches at the same irresistible pace every time.

Passage is a *memento mori* – a game created in order to remind us that we will die. And, because to many people that will seem an exceedingly strange thing for a video game to do, Jason Rohrer has devoted a page of his website to explaining exactly why he made it. 'It presents an entire life, from young adulthood through old age and death, in the span of five minutes,' he writes. 'Of course, it's a *game*, not a painting or a film, so the choices that you make as the player are crucial. There's no "right" way to play *Passage*, just as there's no right way to interpret it. However, I had specific intentions for the various mechanics and features that I included.'

'As you age in the game, your character moves closer and closer to the right edge of the screen. Upon reaching that edge, your character [a tiny male figure] dies.' Appropriately enough, the further along in your life you are, the more you are able to see behind you and the less ahead. Then, there's your spouse, who you can choose either to walk into and join with, or simply avoid. 'You have the option of joining up with a spouse on your journey ... Once you team up with her, however, you must travel together, and you are not as agile as you were when you were single. Some rewards deep in the maze will no longer be reachable if you're with your spouse. You simply cannot fit through narrow paths when you are walking side-by-side ... On the other hand, exploring the world is more enjoyable with a companion, and you'll reap a larger reward from exploration if she's along. When she dies, though, your grief will slow you down considerably.' Finally, there remain the points in the top right-hand corners, which you're free to expend as much or as little effort as you like collecting. Although, as Rohrer notes, it's a mission his game loads with a cold irony. 'In the end, death is still coming for you. Your score looks pretty meaningless hovering there above your little tombstone . . . *Passage* is a game in which you die only once, at the very end, and you are power-less to stave off this inevitable loss.'

Passage is a sad, modest, brilliant game, and one that achieves its effects entirely without the aid of a script or anything but the most rudimentary sounds and visuals. It's an experience that can only be appreciated by the actual process of play – that simply couldn't be said in any other way. Within a medium that as a whole is so unabashedly a form of mass market entertain-ment, it's also a wonderful example of something that many people simply don't believe exists: the avant-garde.

Financially, this is certainly pretty insignificant. Culturally, though, it is a sign of perhaps the most welcome revelation of all, that gaming is an arena where players' and designers' passions can flow along channels as unabashedly ambitious and intellec-tually bold as they have always done in the other creative arts. This is not a medium that is automatically debarred from engaging with the great, enduring human questions, even if it chooses to do so in miniature rather than epic form.

Jason Rohrer doesn't prove this on his own, of course. But the milieu to which he belongs is just beginning to come into its own in the online realm of freely distributed browser-based and downloadable games. It's a realm of often wild, delightful innovations and deeply considered discussions, where miniature games programmed as labours of love by one or two coders can model everything from time-travelling robots (*Chronotron*) to interactive single screens where a woman in a rowing boat falls in love with a young man sitting on the moon (*I wish I were the moon*). It's also, most encouragingly of all, connected to the mainstream of gaming by a constant exchange of talent, play-time, uploads, downloads and pet projects that form a creative ecosystem most other media can only watch with mounting envy.

At the other end of the scale, there are different ways in which games are pushing at – and redefining – the limits of their poten-tial as a creative medium. The sector is usually referred to as 'hard-core' gaming and includes those titles whose challenges and mechanics are designed to appeal to those with literally thousands of hours of gaming experience under their belts. This can just be a question of unforgiving difficulty, or frenetic action of the most unreflective kind. But it can also be something rather more elaborate – and can, especially in the online world, test the potential of video games not only as artistic creations in their own right, but as mechanisms via which players themselves create and take part in a kind of art.

If *Flower* and *Passage* are the poetry of the game world, the massively multiplayer game EVE *Online* is the *Finnegans Wake* of video gaming, requiring many hundreds of hours of effort if you wish even to begin to grasp its intricacies, and typically demanding a good fifty hours of input before you can start to work out what the true focus and dynamics of the game are. EVE is a game of space exploration and trading, and is currently played by over 300,000 people, all of whom inhabit the same virtual galaxy, a place located in the distant future that contains over 7,500 star systems, each with their own planets, moons and space stations.

The basics of the game are a complex matter of learning to fly and equip a spaceship, performing a variety of missions for cash and reputation, gaining wealth and raw materials, exploration, and so on. All these must be mastered before the game's true heart can be glimpsed: the political and economic manoeuvrings that take place between the vast shifting alliances of players within the game. Much of EVE's richness – and its almost absurd complexity – lies in the twisting history of betrayals, wars, blood feuds and communitarian endeavours that comprise the history of players' actions over the course of the seven years that the EVE galaxy has existed.

If EVE is art, the genre it's most closely aligned to is performance art, with the emergent behaviours and narratives that players themselves have created over time providing a far richer context than any script. One incident that's still talked about to this day is a 'heist' in 2005 in which, over a period of twelve months, one specialist alliance of covert assassins, the Guiding Hand Social Club, infiltrated every level of one of the game's most powerful player-run corporations, the Ubiqua Seraph. The corporation CEO herself flew an ultra-rare ship of which only two known examples existed in the EVE universe, while it controlled a staggering quantity of in-game assets valued at tens of thousands of real-world dollars. The signal was given, and a deadly coordinated attack by the infiltrators wiped out within a matter of hours the CEO herself, her ship, and over $15,000 worth of corporate assets. It was a masterpiece of espionage and planning for which a lucrative in-game contract had been taken out, and was duly paid, by a rival corporation. And it was all entirely within the rules and spirit of the game. In fact, such a plot – involving many hundreds of people unfolding over the best part of a year – was exactly what EVE had been created to facilitate.

In the context of both modern media and the arts, the fact that games are a live, shared performance is an increasingly crucial one. First mass production and now mass distribution have had a substantial impact on our relationship with the whole notion of art. Sitting in front of a screen connected to the internet today, it is so easy to browse or purchase a good proportion of all the books ever written, to listen to a similar amount of recorded music and speech, to view images of the finest two-and-three dimensional art in the world's great museums, to purchase or stream films and television, and so on. Things have never been simpler for those who are content to experience art as a medley of facsimiles, digital copies and searchable text – or harder for those who wish to have confidence in any one object as a meaningful, definitive artistic experience.

This is why live experiences of all kinds have made such a comeback in recent years. From classic bands reforming to go on tour to blockbusting art exhibitions and literary festivals, live art is at an unprecedented premium in an age of cheap, rapid distribution; because it's seeing something in the flesh, in the present tense, that allows people to feel a connection of authenticity and value, rather than watch it wash over them as just another undifferentiated part of the global information tide.

Video games are thoroughly digital, mass-produced objects. Yet they cannot be consumed passively. To consume a game is by definition to experience it, from moment to moment, as a gradual encounter with a space and a set of ideas; and the art form it most resembles in this respect is one that came to prominence at almost exactly the same time as the first mass-market video games – installation art. One of the world's finest, and most staggeringly successful, spaces for such art is the Turbine Hall of the Tate Modern museum in London. With 3,400 square metres of floor space and five storeys of height, the Turbine Hall is one of the most striking settings for art in the world and, since it was opened in 2000, it has hosted installations including huge stacks of white boxes, a gigantic crack in the floor, an indoors weather system complete with mist and sunshine, and a series of giant steel slides which visitors were encouraged to use. It's easy enough to see the analogy with a video game here: a realm is marked out as distinct from the rest of the world, as a kind of playground for the senses and the mind; and it's each individual's gradual experience and exploration of this space that conjures up its artistic meaning.

It would be foolish to push this analogy too far. And yet, increasingly, the connection between video games and some other important, real-world forms of art is becoming a two-way street. Take one of the most talked-about British theatrical ventures of recent years: the Punchdrunk theatre company, who have staged several hugely popular and critically acclaimed shows in which the audience, rather than sitting passively in front of a live show, are forced to discover the performance they are attending by exploring a particular building or location. The idea of audience interaction is hardly new, but in the hands of Punchdrunk it has taken on an entirely different dimension. Their 2009 show *Tunnel 228*, for example, simply abandoned its audience in a subterranean network of cellars and caverns beneath London's Waterloo station with little sense of direction or clue as to what was going on. Industrial machinery and disturbing fragments of performance art were scattered around, together with elliptical private codes and clues that most of the audience would never even discover. But the experience was, deliberately, a combination of puzzle, treasure hunt and survival horror.

It's theatrical immersion of the most disturbing, gripping kind, and, as *Time Out* features writer and critic (and sometime Punchdrunk groupie) Peter Watts observed in his own writings on the topic, it's also, well, more than a little like a video game. All the tropes are there. They had 'a sinister, self-enclosed world; atmospheric sound and light; the freedom to explore a vast Tardis-like world within tightly-defined borders; the concept that you have a central "mission" to fulfil, but also the liberty to ignore it if the mood strikes you; the secret doors and curtains concealing hidden treasures, imaginatively created.' The *Tunnel 228* experience, if not directly inspired by video games, nevertheless shares with them an aesthetic that, like cinema a century ago, has begun to seep out of its original context into art and society as a whole. This is the aesthetic of the interactive space: the audience-generated narrative; the careful mixing of freedom with constraint into a new kind of performance.

It's become an increasingly common practice in recent years to dismiss the worst and most vacuous kinds of art in other media – in cinema, on television, even in books – as 'like video games'. What's usually meant by this is a mindless kind of frenzy: anaesthetising, undifferentiated action involving metal, muscles and guns. Some games do look like this from the outside – and the worst ones play like it, too. But this is a brand of criticism that couldn't be further from the truth. The frenzy isn't a sign that games are debasing all other arts to an unprecedented creative depth; it's a sign that many film-makers, producers and publishers have little concept of what makes the best games so great, or of where the artistic merits of their own media lie. Video games have barely begun to demonstrate their potential, yet already they are changing the way we see the world – and how we conceive ourselves within it.

CHAPTER 8

Second lives

In September 2009, the first-ever licensed use of the music of the Beatles outside of their own albums and compilations arrived in the form of – what else? – a video game. *The Beatles: Rock Band* was released to what can only be described as hysterical approval and represents the peak, so far, of one of the youngest and most astonishingly successful trends in gaming – its encroachment not only into the music industry, but into the whole notion of lifestyle and media consumption, in a manner far broader and more powerful than anything ever considered the terrain of a 'game'.

The *Rock Band* games, of which there are now five (plus six expansion 'track packs') are essentially an extremely sophisticated offshoot of multimedia karaoke. Players accompany hit songs on vocals, guitars and drums, and are awarded points and feedback for the quality of their performance. It sounds standard enough. Yet, in these games, popular music is being made available for consumption in a form that has never existed before: an interactive form, broken down by instruments and vocals, and complete with a sophisticated interface that will train listeners

135

to play along with every note, record and grade their every effort, and allow them and their friends to get about as close as is humanly possible to the experience of being, for the length of one track, a member of the Beatles.

Rock Band makes an MP3 recording seem about as limiting and primitive as a wax disk. Along with other similar titles like the *Guitar Hero* and *SingStar* series, it has already revolutionised the music market, having achieved over a billion dollars of sales, 50 million song downloads and 10 million copies sold. And that's just the *Rock Band* games – and it's also just the beginning. For the experience these products can offer in comparison to traditional media is simply unrivalled. In an age where the cost of non-interactive media is rapidly tending towards zero, it suggests that such innovations should be pretty much irresistible to any company wanting to offer their consumers a service they can actually charge for. Think of what a customer now expects from even an up-to-date television service. Simply being able to flick between a hundred, or even a thousand, channels is no longer enough. Users expect programmes on-demand; an up-to-date programme schedule and information service; the option of recording and rewinding multiple programmes, of organising their recordings, and setting them days or weeks in advance; they expect to be able to manage their account options, hardware configuration, software set-up and preferences. None of this is a game in any strict sense, yet this is a distinction which is becoming more blurred by the day; for, in every aspect of interaction, it's video games above all that are both defining expectations and setting the standard for new technology.

Games, moreover, are becoming a seriously revolutionary force for many more fields than music. Take the 2009 game *Ghostbusters*, a product whose relationship with the two hit 1980s *Ghostbusters* films is a little more complex than the old school formula of a bit of interactive shooting and exploring dressed up in images from the film. For a start, the game itself is based around an original script part-written by Dan Aykroyd and Harold Ramis (who wrote and starred in the films) and features the vocal talents of the original cast, not to mention motion-captured computer recreations of their 1980s appearances and an exact reproduction of the musical score. The banter and visuals, in fact, are of a standard that comfortably exceeds many beloved movies of the 1980s and, much like the game's budget of over $15 million, it's difficult not to see the finished product as far more than simply the 'game of the films'. As Aykroyd himself put it in one interview, 'I've seen work on the video game, I've watched it progress, my rap now to people is "This is essentially the third movie".'

Looking ahead to the not-too-distant future, it's not hard to imagine a time when the Blu-Ray release of a blockbuster film may also contain a video game, and even integrate the two. Consumers still want the passive viewing experience but, when the mood takes them, they expect to be able to launch into interaction at a moment's notice. The point at which a game experience ends and another kind of experience begins may become difficult to pinpoint.

It's a point that hasn't been lost on Steven Spielberg, who in 2008 was credited as the lead designer on a new video game,

Boom Blox, for the Nintendo Wii. Would this be a cinematic epic, bringing his storytelling gifts and visual flair to the living-room screen in an unprecedented interactive form? Far from it. The game actually presented an abstract – and extremely playable – series of physics-based puzzles, involving knocking down piles of blocks. Designing *Boom Blox* was, Spielberg explained in an interview in 2008, driven by the desire 'to get parents and kids in the same space together'. It also involved, he noted, the virtualisation of one of the most ancient and most elemental kinds of childhood play – 'knocking blocks down'.

Spielberg's construction of this kind of shared space is both a significant achievement in itself, and a development that points towards far bigger changes – the increasing power of video games not only as a product to be consumed, but as a state of mind or place to be visited.

If you want to understand what it means to lead a 'gaming life', there are few better people to talk to than Nick Yee. An American games researcher whose projects have over the best part of the last decade pooled an unrivalled quantity of data on players' shifting experiences of gaming in the modern world, Yee has, he explains to me, three 'prongs of research'. The first has involved surveying over 70,000 online gamers about their behaviour and attitudes. The second has used immersive virtual reality technology to test how people interact in virtual environments. And the third involves 'data mining' from the servers of companies running MMOs – and then matching players' opinions of their own behaviour with the mass of detailed data being kept by the companies operating the games they're playing. Such a considerable information package has earned him a doctorate from Stanford and international renown in the gaming and academic communities, but it has also thrown up one persistent contradiction: that much of what people do when they play video games looks like very hard work – despite their claims that it represents the precise opposite.

Yee was first struck a couple of years ago by players' behaviour within an online game set in one of the most famous futuristic science-fiction worlds ever created, *Star Wars Galaxies*. By any other name, what was taking place within the game was not just the kind of advanced cooperation or competition traditionally associated with play, but full-on corporate and individual enterprise. 'The use of the business metaphor was dominant among players,' he explains. This wasn't so much about teaming up to kill ultra-tough enemies as about what happened around the margins of more traditional kinds of 'play': the processing and maximising of in-game raw resources, the determined exploitation of player markets. 'There were these groups of people who were collecting raw resources, doing research, manufacturing products on an open market, finding clever ways of advertising to other players. For a lot of players, their game time was literally like a second job.'

One example Yee uses to explain exactly what he means is the in-game profession of 'pharmaceutical manufacturing' in *Star Wars Galaxies*: an ability that involves processing raw materials such as chemicals and minerals. These materials are bought from other players, who have in turn harvested them using their skills at geological surveying and mining. Taking advantage of economies of scale, resources tend to be bought from players who specialise in bulk-buying and can thus supply at low prices. Once bought, materials have to be processed within factories (that have to be built by players skilled as architects). All of these skills have to be laboriously trained up from scratch by the repetition of various, increasingly complex tasks. For a lot of players, this kind of 'second job' involves a staggering amount of what looks like ritual tedium: logging on daily to check in with their client base, ensuring sales orders are all going out on time, checking the state of the market, purchasing materials at the best possible price, and so on.

'It was something that really made me rethink what was happening with the work involved in dragon-slaying in other games,' Yee told me. The fantasy scenarios of the most popular online games – involving wizards, elves, orcs and goblins – automatically make them seem escapist. Yet, beneath the surface things are happening that are increasingly difficult to encompass within the word 'game' in any traditional sense. As Yee points out, the kinds of tasks undertaken by many players 'involve an awful lot of work: the logistical management of maybe a hundred people in different time zones, keeping everyone happy in a group with ages ranging from twelve to sixty. I found that there were people burning out from MMOs just like they do from high-pressure jobs.'

Yee's research may sound like it is dealing in extreme examples, yet the convergence of real life with game-playing it suggests is at work to a lesser degree across a whole spectrum of gaming activities. One of the other areas he has investigated is the relationship between players' attitudes towards games and the real world. He experimented by putting people 'into' different kinds of avatars using virtual reality goggles, which made them feel like they're actually inside an admittedly fairly crude virtual world. Subjects were put into more and less attractive kinds of virtual body, and left to interact. The results showed that people put into more attractive avatars were bolder within the virtual world, and were prepared to walk closer to virtual strangers – a predictable enough result, except that Yee then arranged a follow-up experiment, taking people who had just completed the VR study and sitting them down in front of a mocked-up dating website. This, they were told, was a different experiment into online dating; the subjects were then shown nine images of the sex they were interested in and asked to pick two they wanted to know more about. 'We found,' Yee told me, 'that people who had been given attractive virtual avatars chose more attractive partners in this online dating task, while those who had been in unattractive avatars picked less attractive partners.'

This is both a limited and a highly suggestive result. It doesn't prove that virtual interactions simply spill over into real ones; but it does suggest that, at least when it comes to the human body, people take into and out of video games a malleable conception of self that doesn't draw a hard line between their actual body and their in-game avatar. The imaginative act of embodiment, when it comes to actually controlling a humanoid character in a virtual world, involves not only a projection but also a temporary blurring of identity, almost as if the player becomes somehow distributed between their actual and their virtual self – neither entirely one nor the other.

Yee uses the example of the virtual world *Second Life* to illustrate this in a little more detail. *Second Life*, he points out, is an environment constructed almost entirely by its players, where people can look like anything they want and build almost anything they want. Yet the most bizarre environmental feature of all is barely commented upon by the world's million-plus users: the fact that it all looks so much like suburban America. 'People spend all their time there shopping for virtual Abercrombie & Fitch knock-offs,' he notes, wonderingly. 'In a world where it is so easy to look beautiful and to rate high in the measures we use in the physical world, I suppose it's really hard not to get seduced by them.'

Second Life itself isn't quite a game; it's a virtual environment without set aims, rules or levels, where people go to interact and express themselves. Yet, as with so many other virtual (and indeed real) environments, the ways in which players themselves use it involves constructing what are effectively a succession of mini-games out of the raw materials on offer: competing to look better, to be more noticeable, but also testing their virtual environment's laws and limits in order to gain advantages over one another, to show off, and to profit from their activities.

One example of just how far this kind of undertaking can go is an altogether more intriguing kind of clothing than ersatz-

Abercrombie: real, physical pairs of jeans that are 'manufactured' from within *Second Life* by a specialist company called Invisible Threads. The concept itself is a strange mix of concept art and e-commerce. Described as a 'mixed reality performance installation', the company was created by the multimedia artists Jeff Crouse and Stephanie Rothenberg for the 2008 Sundance Film Festival. Since then, however, it's taken on something of a life of its own, growing into an increasingly prophetic demonstration of the remarkably interchangeable ideas of virtual play and real-life work.

The process begins with customers ordering their jeans at a real, physical kiosk. Prices are given in both real-world dollars and the convertible house currency of *Second Life*, the Linden Dollar, and start at about US $32 or around 8,000 Linden Dollars, for a classic pair – not bad at all by designer standards. This order is then broadcast live by camera and microphone into a virtual sweatshop, a sturdy virtual building on a private island within *Second Life*. Over the next few minutes, the customer can watch onscreen in real time as the product is put together by a team of *Second Life* workers: avatars controlled by real *Second Life* players who have answered in-game job adverts offering to pay them a wage of just under one (real) dollar an hour to work in the jeans factory.

Each virtual worker has an individual station within the virtual factory, at which they process a particular detail of the customer's unique specifications: size, design, requested customisations, stitching details and so on. In a cunningly Orwellian innovation, the video of the customer is projected across a whole wall of the virtual factory, and everything is performed in real time. The actual people controlling these workers are, of course, seated variously around the world, watching events unfold on their screens. At the end, after a quality control worker has ensured the virtual object is up to standard, the finished item then passes into a 'Second Life/Real Life portal' which transports it into the real world. What this means in practice is that the jeans emerge as a life-size schematic printout from a special printer in the real-world sales kiosk. The schematic is used as a template for rapid assembly from existing rolls of fabric, which are cut out and stuck together on the spot by a sales assistant. And the customer walks away wearing their new jeans.

The whole enterprise is above all intended to bend traditional boundaries and assumptions about the manufacturing process and its relation to space, labour and geography. Yet, as its creators noted in an interview after the Sundance festival, this integration of real and unreal environments 'not only sheds light on the current politics of outsourced labour but foreshadows what has already become the future of capitalist production'. For example – amazingly enough – the margins involved in making and selling a pair of jeans like this are pretty good. Both land and labour within virtual environments can, for a start, be bought at a fraction of the cost of their physical equivalents – and you can leverage the skills of a workforce based in as many or as few countries as you choose. Paying workers 90 cents an hour is generous by *Second Life* standards (an added incentive is the fact that each worker is granted some virtual land next to the factory to build themselves a shack) and, apart from the salary of the sixteen workers involved, other costs are minimal. Materials and printing cost just a few dollars; assembly takes only a few unskilled minutes with glue and basic stitching.

Perhaps most intriguing of all is the fact that people are willing, and even eager, to 'work' like this within a world whose entire purpose is supposed to be leisure, and that defines itself as a playful refuge from the pressures of real life. What people appear to be enjoying here is essentially an idealised version of the satisfactions granted by work: camaraderie, team-work, concrete achievement, improved skills. By comparison, it seems, aimless leisure is dull – one of the reasons that *Second Life's* citizens seek out such activities, and that *Second Life* itself is far outstripped in popularity by the purpose-driven realm of out-and-out online games. Where, then, is the work/leisure dichotomy so central to much of our recent cultural history?

It might seem that the waters couldn't get much muddier than virtual jeans manufacture in terms of the divisions between play, pleasure, work and leisure. But even the playful production of real goods has its counterpoint, with as much real-life work being expended on creating virtual items for game worlds as virtual work is expended on creating real ones. The key – and now infamous – phrase here is 'gold farming', a global phenomenon that's driven entirely by video games, and stemming from one simple fact: with tens of millions of people playing online games around the world, there is now a huge global demand for supplies of virtual currency to service these players' online adventuring habits.

145

Most video games, unlike *Second Life*-style virtual worlds, deliberately don't allow their players to leverage their real-world wealth by buying in-game currency: this would grossly unbalance their economies and power structures, and make the entire game experience less fun for everyone. The only way to obtain in-game currency, then, is to perform in-game tasks. But the last thing that many players want to do is spend tens or hundreds of hours of their own time grinding away to get enough virtual cash for a particular sword, steed, shield or whatever. And so, in the time-honoured tradition of supply and demand, they pay other, real people with real money to earn virtual cash for them.

The industry is known as gold farming because 'gold' is the most common name for virtual currency in online games, and 'farming' is an especially apt metaphor for the set routines that it's necessary to perform for hour after hour within an online game in order to earn said gold. Statistics are necessarily sketchy, but it's undoubtedly a booming sector. At its global heart, in China, some estimates put the number of gold farmers at close to a million people and their annual trading at close to $10 billion; certainly, the global figure should be thought of in billions rather than millions.

Twenty years ago, this would have sounded like the most extreme kind of satire, had you attempted to describe it, and yet the economic logic behind gold farming is as sound as that behind any kind of outsourcing – or, indeed, behind operating a sweatshop in *Second Life*. The amount that consumers will pay for the product, less the effort and expense it takes to make it, equals profit; and it's neither here nor there, in at least these fundamental terms, that the product in question has no existence beyond bits of data on a number of computers owned and operated by a video games company. A typical 'cottage gold farming' outfit in China involves a team of workers living together in a dormitory and working in a rented room full of computers for an effective wage of 30 cents per hour. In this rented room, they will play a game – usually *World of Warcraft*, thanks to the size and affluence of its player market – for twelve hours a night, seven days a week. They will battle through precise areas and tasks again and again, pulling in virtual gold which will then be sold by their local employer to an online retailer for around $3 per hundred gold coins. Because the gold cannot exist independently of a game account, the sale will mean that both parties must have their own game characters, and will use the in-game player-to-player mailing system to transfer the gold. These hundred coins will then be sold for up to $20 to a Western player, via one of the numerous websites specialising in such transactions – and the coins will duly arrive in the player's in-game mail box. Such transactions are, naturally, explicitly against the rules of the game as defined by its operators.

As you might expect, endless variations exist on this theme, some far more profitable and sophisticated than others. You can pay for someone else to build you a character from scratch. You can buy characters at a particular level and of a particular class for your friends. You can even pay a team of twenty-five virtual mercenaries to take you along as a passenger through the toughest dungeon in the game, and get to pick up every single piece of treasure for yourself along the way. It sounds crazy, and doesn't come cheap, but given that the world is already collectively spending over forty billion legal dollars on video games annually, this kind of secondary expenditure has a whiff of inevitability about it.

What does it all signify, though, beyond the fact that some people are only too happy to profit from others taking play very seriously? The New York-based author and technology journalist Julian Dibbell has spent more time than most plumbing the depths of virtual and real-world interactions. He has been writing about video gaming since the early 1990s, but it was in 2003 that he took his most radical step into testing where the boundaries between modern work and electronic play might lie, deciding that he would spend a year attempting to earn a living wage, in America, entirely by trading in virtual items found within the game *Ultima Online*. It was an endeavour he recorded in a book, *Play Money* (2006), and culminated in the conclusion that he could earn around $3,000 a month, working no more than fifty hours a week, entirely by trading in-game items.

What was it like to spend so much time in an ephemeral realm, working entirely with objects that had no real-life counterparts, I asked? It was, he explained, a bizarrely rooted existence in many ways, compare to the vagaries of the real world's money markets. 'The irony is that, compared to the financial derivatives that got puffed into a bubble and burst in 2008, these virtual economies and these virtual monies are much more solidly founded and robust. People say that this virtual trade is the ultimate culmination of high capitalist economics, where all that is solid melts into air and money is based on nothingness. Yet, if you look at what is actually going on in these games, there is something much more solid there than what's happening in financial markets. This virtual gold has real value because people have real attachments to it: and not just to the games, but to the other people that are in them.'

When someone in America pays $100 to a website to buy some virtual gold that has taken a Chinese person 100 hours to earn, it's certainly difficult to treat the leisure of the one and the labour of the other as two different orders of activity. The American will even go out and do, for pleasure (and while paying for the privilege), almost exactly the same thing as the Chinese person has just done for a subsistence wage. The only real difference is the element of choice. And yet, even here, the boundaries are far from clear-cut. As Dibbell discovered while investigating the world of Chinese gold farming on location (something that he detailed for the *New York Times* magazine in June 2007), even in the depths of a twelve-hour daily *World of Warcraft* grind, a Chinese worker could say that he felt a 'playful attitude' towards what he was doing. Or there was the ten-man team of 'power levellers' who Dibbell observed choosing, with only one exception, to spend their few waking hours of free time in the very same game that they were working themselves to the bone playing for money: *World of Warcraft*.

One key aspect of this staggering motivational capability is what's known as a 'reward schedule' – that is, a carefully tailored timetable governing the rate at which different kinds of rewards are given to players as they progress through a game. At the start, when a lot of basic learning is likely to be going on and a player doesn't yet have much invested in the game, the rewards will come close together: more powers, graphical effects, new equipment, a higher character level, new areas to explore, and so on. Gradually, then, these rewards will become further and further apart, with a tantalising random element included to keep players guessing (and hopeful) and plenty of distractions and mini-objectives to keep them committed. If it's sufficiently well designed and, most importantly, thoroughly tested and refined, a player will suddenly discover that it now takes two days rather than two hours to raise their character by one more level – but that they're quite willing to invest the time needed to progress further.

There is a certain level of paradox here: that, in a well-made game, the more fun someone is having, the harder they work. It's almost as if a video game is not only something that delivers fun by satisfying the innate human love of learning, but also a device that trains people to work far harder than they otherwise would by turning work into a series of tangibly rewarded learning challenges.

This motivational power is something Nick Yee has explored in his work, citing in particular the example of a behavioural economics study in which people were given the option of doing 'a really boring task' for either half an hour or an hour. They weren't to be paid for their time as such; instead, half an hour meant earning 30 points, while an hour meant 100 points. These points could then be spent on ice cream, according to two rules:

100 points awarded pistachio flavour and 30 points awarded vanilla. Most of the undergraduates taking part decided to work for an hour in order to get 100 points and thus the pistachio ice cream. Yet, when the experimenters went back and asked what kind of ice cream they preferred, most people turned out to prefer vanilla. It sounds like a trivial enough observation, but it illustrates just how powerful a motivator even a completely arbitrary scoring system can be. It's a little like magic, after all, to persuade a room full of people to work for twice as long as they need to in order to earn a reward that most of them don't like as much as the one they would have got had they worked for half that amount of time.

This is the kind of magic at which video games excel beyond anything else. It is a medium in which, quite literally, one kind of value is conjured out of thin air while – almost unnoticed – the certainty of most other kinds is whisked away. It is a kind of magic that has an unusually close relationship with another ultimately arbitrary scoring system that exists only because of human consensus: money itself. What is money, after all, if not a shared fiction maintained to allow the exchange, purchase and valuation of real goods and services independently of their actual nature? As the recent financial crisis has demonstrated, money is a fiction that can all too easily take on many of the characteristics of farce. Yet many of the greatest changes to the way we think about value, effort and exchange in the future are likely to come not from the increasingly abstract activities of lenders and spenders dealing in vast sums, but from a far more basic set of principles relating to what ordinary people actually attach value to and decide to spend their time pursuing. As online games have already begun to demonstrate, millions of people are barely able to put an upper limit on the worth of certain kinds of fun; and it's this economics of pleasure and leisure rather than of labour that has perhaps the greatest lessons to teach us about the coming century.

CHAPTER 9

Serious play

In 2007, the Serious Games Institute was founded at Coventry University in England. The name, which sounds like a contradiction in terms, signalled the Institute's commitment to studying video games' potential uses across a spectrum of 'serious' activities: games as learning and training tools, as educational aids, as a means of social and political engagement, and so on. Under the aegis of its founding director David Wortley, however, the Institute has also developed a strong emphasis on understanding some of the larger principles underpinning modern gaming – and on exploring what lessons games might hold for the realms of business and public service, not to mention their broader philosophical and sociological implications.

It's a field that lies on the periphery of the modern games industry; nevertheless, a gathering body of research into the kind of lessons that might be drawn from video gaming globally is starting to hold out the prospect of quite transforming discoveries, both in enterprise and in the more nebulous region of the social and psychological sciences.

Wortley's own background is far from traditional for the games industry. For a start, there's his age: at nearly sixty, he has several decades on most of even his more venerable peers. Moreover, although he has always worked with technology, his long career is rooted in the world of business rather than entertainment: first as an electronic engineer, then as a manager for the British Post Office, an IBM marketing executive, an information technology entrepreneur and, now, an academic and researcher.

There are, Wortley believes, two common attributes emerging in the interconnected spheres of social networks, games and virtual worlds that are absolutely crucial to the future of twenty-first-century business. First, there is the notion of personalisation: games and online social networks have between them transformed the expectations of an entire generation in their dealings with technology. Wortley explains, 'For the first time ever, people interacting with a computer are able to personalize their own space. They genuinely feel they have something individual to them which they can shape.' Second, there is the related concept of persistence: the fact that people now expect a virtual environment to have many of the properties of a real, miniature world, with its own continuing existence independent of its users logging on or off. 'With a persistent environment, when you go back in, it remembers where you were before: what you did, the assets and marks you created, your achievements. There is a kind of mirror image of the real world that you can create for yourself.'

Between them, these points represent something that the traditional computing and communications industries – for all the billions of dollars spent every year on research and development – often do badly or not at all. Computers and operating systems within business, for example, are almost entirely static as work environments. Every time you turn a computer off or exit an individual program, while you may save individual files and settings, there is no sense that you are moving into and out of a truly customisable environment that goes on existing in your absence, and that can be fundamentally modified in its appearance and behaviour to suit your preferences and needs. There is no sense that you have a permanent, individual space on your computer where work can be shared and ideas discussed; nor, when you are away can other people see exactly what you have been working on. Compared to a MySpace or Facebook page, let alone a character or location in a virtual world, most computers are about as dynamic as the fabric of the building they're sitting in.

In addition to these failings, most non-entertainment programs on computers – from word processing to databases or email clients – remain dauntingly hard to master to the uninitiated. This is because they rely on a set of conventions that seem simple enough when memorised, but that have little intuitive logic to them; for example, the fact that the 'File' menu in most Microsoft programs contains the 'Exit' command is almost impossible to reason out except by trial and error or the laborious consultation of search documents. Indeed, the whole system of drop-down menus driven by key words like 'Edit' and 'Tools' is hardly a model of self-explanatory usability, despite years of efforts to improve it.

In an age in which digital literacy is essential within most workplaces, it may sound trivial to worry about such basics; but anyone who has either had to explain how, say, an internet browser works to a non-technical relative, or who has suddenly found themselves required to start using an entirely new suite of software applications, will have a keen understanding of just how impenetrable are the webs of conventions surrounding many computing activities. Even explaining the notion of a 'double click' with a mouse – and helping someone who has never done it before to double click on an icon – reveals how surprisingly tricky some of the most basic acts associated with using a computer still are.

This is where games come in. Games companies, after all, spend literally billions of dollars on ensuring that their products are easy to use and accessible to a degree inconceivable in most corporate products. No one is being paid to play a game, and so the designers must ensure that at every stage users are drawn in and trained to understand the game systems without even noticing. There are no double clicks in game worlds, and no incomprehensible menus; at least, not in successful titles, whose creators' philosophies tend to be that anyone who's interested ought to be guided by the gradual structure of a game into knowing exactly how to use an often highly complicated set of skills.

As Wortley puts it, 'emerging interface technologies are largely being driven by the games industry; and it's this that will ultimately change the way that people interact with technology'. And 'emerging interface technologies' include, in the case of products like the Nintendo Wii or the *Guitar Hero* games (which use a plastic guitar as their principal control method), highly innovative ways of interacting with computers that lie well outside the traditional bounds of a keyboard, mouse and monitor. Wortley himself confesses, 'When I play games, it's mainly *Guitar Hero* for me. Prior to that, I always found the console interface unfriendly to someone of my generation. But I saw this game in PC World, thought it was worth trying and got completely hooked. This combination of the way it uses the interface and has a great design and is incredibly intuitive just to pick up and play is a fantastic example of best practice for anyone: a balance of accessibility, challenge, reward, making people want to progress and develop their skills, to learn and train.'

Games have long been one of the world's most important engines for computing innovation – along with, more recently, the mobile phone. It's largely thanks to the ever-evolving ambitions of game designers that modern computers have a DVD drive, a graphics card, decent sound capability, a staggering amount of RAM, a large colour monitor, and so on. None of this, technically, is required for word processing or even for producing presentations; the multi-media PC is very much a child of gaming, and has been since its youngest days. Now, though, with the power and speed of even inexpensive modern computers at an unprecedented level in historical terms, games designers have begun to turn to perfecting the field of access and interface design – to help as many people as possible to perform complex tasks on a machine in a manner that is engaging and intuitive.

Consider the standard physical interface between a user and a computer. In an age where the phone in most pockets is smarter than the computer that put men on the moon, the keyboards we type on are essentially identical not only to those used on the very first home computers, but to nineteenth-century typewriters. It's a bit like using reins to drive an F1 car. Even the mouse has hardly changed in more than twenty-five years. Keyboards and mice are still with us because they work very well, if you know how to use them, and because of a momentum within the computing industry itself: like the arrangement of letters on a keyboard, they have become too familiar and ubiquitous simply to sweep away – attempts to transform or replace them in the past have invariably foundered. Yet, in recent years, the serious possibility of an interface revolution has begun to arise, thanks almost entirely to advances made in the gaming sector (and thanks to its need to woo its audience with pleasure rather than bludgeon it with obligations).

Motion sensitivity, above all in the form of Nintendo's controllers for its Wii console, is the most successful mass market innovation to have come from this field, but much more radical devices are not far behind. One especially impressive example is a device known as a NeuroSky. Worn like an elaborate pair of headphones, it allows the user to control an electronic device with the power of their mind – purely by concentrating, and without moving physically in any way. It may sound like science fiction, yet it is already available to purchase for around $200, and can be used off the shelf: users simply attach the headset, start concentrating, and let the 'dry neural sensor technology' read and interpret activity in the brain through the skin.

Perhaps inevitably, the first application to show off the

NeuroSky was a delightfully tacky-looking game known as the *Star Wars Force Trainer*, in which a sphere can be moved up and down within a 'training tower' simply by thinking about it (as demonstrated at a recent games conference by a large man in a Darth Vader outfit). As ever in the history of computing, if a company wants to engage an audience's imagination and show off the interactive potentials of a technology to its best ability, a game is an unrivalled demonstration tool.

Aside from brain waves, less than $200 could also buy a Novint Falcon controller, which replaces the standard mouse with a ping-pong ball-sized device, attached by three supporting arms to a series of sensors and motors housed in a weighted base. It looks like a slightly dangerous toy robot, but the Novint Falcon is in fact one of an increasing number of 'haptic devices' on the market: interfaces that provide direct physical feedback from what's onscreen, such as giving a sense of recoil to in-game guns or allowing users to experience the weight of virtual objects. The Novint Falcon was developed for the mass market in the gaming sector, which remains its main source of revenues, but it actually began its existence as a tool to help doctors perform examinations remotely. In combination with other forms of motion sensitivity, the potential for serious as well as entertainment uses for such innovations is vast. This is true, too, of those less able to use the traditional keyboard and mouse, either because of inexperience, age, infirmity or disability; already, it's arguable that Nintendo's Wii has done more to bring the power of computing to new kinds of users than anything since the birth of the internet itself.

In addition to all these innovations, there's the equally enticing possibility of revolutionising not just how we interact with what's on a screen, but how the contents of that screen appear to us. One enterprising graduate student, Johnny Chung Lee, at Carnegie Mellon University, has, for instance, already demonstrated that an adapted Wii controller can be combined with a computer, television and two LED lights to function as an extremely effective virtual reality display. The LED lights are worn on an adapted pair of goggles attached to your head, allowing the sensor to track your motion precisely within a room. The computer then adapts the image on the television depending on where you're standing, meaning that the screen functions exactly as though you were looking through a window into another three-dimensional world. It's an uncanny, and extremely convincing, effect, achievable at negligible cost.

Beyond physical interfaces and appearances, the potential uses of persistent virtual worlds extend well beyond the mere provision of expertise and innovation for other industries. Wortley uses the example, here, of 'intelligent shared spaces'. These entail equipping a physical space, such as an office building, with an array of sensors and monitors that allow its environment to be visualised and managed in real time within a virtual world. Effectively, you have a virtual office whose temperature, lighting, appliances and so on you can manipulate to your heart's content on a computer screen – while all the interactive variables you see, and all the changes you choose to make, are instantly reflected in the actual place.

The technology, Wortley explains, allows designers 'to build intelligence into physical spaces like buildings, so that when you enter somewhere, the building is capable of recognising you, knowing something about you and your interests, how you use the building, what people you are connected to, what you are interested in seeing'. Because everything can be visualised and managed in real time, it allows people the kind of control over – and understanding of – complicated real environments that they have previously extended to virtual ones. If there's one thing that games have demonstrated over the last thirty years, it's that people have an extraordinary aptitude for managing the use of resources within real-time systems, so long as they have suitably clear data, visuals and interfaces – something the games industry has an unrivalled expertise in providing.

This kind of set-up is no pipe dream; it's already being made a reality by people like Swiss entrepreneur Oliver Goh, who's working in partnership with the Coventry Serious Games Institute to bring intelligent shared spaces to life. Goh's product uses a combination of sensor technologies and three-dimensional visualisation to create a system known as 'OpenShaspa', which allows you, as his website explains, to 'monitor and maintain your real life environment via mobile, web, or a 3D space'. Perhaps the simplest and most enticing application of Goh's technology to date is something called the OpenShaspa Home Energy Kit, which displays in real time a household's usage of water, gas and electricity, broken down by individual rooms and appliances within a virtual model of the building. At the click of a mouse, from thousands of miles away (or from the computer in your living room), you can use it to adjust and refine the state of every device in a home – and instantly see the changes to your energy costs. The OpenShaspa kit even includes a 'Social Energy Meter', which makes all your data publicly available online via systems like Google and Facebook; other people can then track, analyse and compare energy patterns across, potentially, local communities, states or even nations.

For many people desperately searching for practical, effective ways of helping ordinary consumers to engage with such crucial yet conceptually daunting environmental issues as energy usage, the kind of lessons this hybrid real/virtual space might yield are invaluable ones. In late 2008, for instance, at the second annual conference on behaviour, energy and climate change in Sacramento, California, Professor Byron Reeves of Stanford University proposed a 'World of Greencraft' scenario. Why stop at the idea of serious games helping people to change their thinking, he argued, when you could go one better than this and turn a householder's own domestic energy consumption into the driving force behind an MMO?

Reeves, an expert in how people process media, produced a demonstration video that showed 'smart' electricity meters in people's homes providing real-time data for virtual versions of their homes online. All these online homes were located within a shared game world in which people could log on as avatars and see each other's virtual dwellings. The game involves incentivising players to compete over having the most energy-efficient virtual home, with the only way to reduce the energy costs of a virtual home being to bring down the energy usage of the actual home. It's a task made easier by in-game information about peak hours of usage, wasteful rooms, appliances and habits, careless oversights, and so on – and the emphasis in the demonstration is firmly on a *Warcraft*-like spirit of competitive cooperation, with local areas teaming up to beat their rivals in having the best statistics.

Reeves's scheme suggests a powerful way of motivating people to take on challenges that have traditionally proved hard to conceptualise, a concept that is sometimes referred to as the art of 'gaming' a particular task or set of ideas. As with many fields, there's little that's fundamentally new about the essential behaviour or techniques involved. People have been 'gaming' life in the pursuit of fun and profit for decades, even for centuries: if you create a fun, rewarding activity within a certain context, you make that context more appealing. From collecting toys in cereal packets to gathering air miles via credit card purchases, it's possible to give an activity 'hooks' – a metaphor that perfectly describes the process of snaring and reeling in users. What video games bring to this field is an unprecedented amount of both information and sophistication. It's an area that few people know better than the American author and researcher Amy Jo Kim, a doctor of behavioural neuroscience and an expert in online community architecture whose work focuses especially on applying game design principles to the wider world.

Jo Kim's approach combines an analysis of our 'primal response patterns' with, once again, the notion of 'flow' – the idea that the right combination of response, challenge and applied skill can induce a heightened, pleasurable state of immersion. She lists five essential mechanisms in the basic gaming process: collecting, points, feedback, exchanges and customisation. One particular case study used by Jo Kim to describe how these features can operate outside of a game setting is YouTube, currently ranked the world's third most popular website after Google and Yahoo! (making it the most-visited web destination in the world unrelated to search). YouTube is in no sense a game, and yet it effortlessly ticks off each of the five gaming mechanisms in turn.

First, collecting: the moment you've created a YouTube account, it's made as easy as possible for you to start gathering up a personal list of 'favourites' that will be displayed to everyone else using the website as part of your public identity, and that allow you to personalise your online space within the site so that, the moment you log on from anywhere in the world, you have at your fingertips everything of value that you've gathered thus far in your use of the site.

Second, points: a simple but absolutely crucial motivator, given the increasingly staggering importance of 'YouTube views' as a public index of the interest and import of any video clip; plus there's the star rating given by users to videos, which provides another incentive for posting and interacting.

Third, feedback: comments posted by other users are an essential part of the atmosphere and the 'stickiness' of the site and, along with the logging of every visit and recommendation, allow people to feel they are part of a dynamic community that can offer both rewards and rebukes to users.

Fourth, exchanges: these are embodied in the feature allowing users to post video responses to other videos, as well as the widespread re-editing and often wholesale reconstruction of other users' videos, turning individual hits into memes that go on being exchanged, repeated, augmented, parodied and paid tribute to for years after they were first posted to the community.

Fifth, customisation: a whole range of options allows users to control what other people see of their tastes and activities, as well as allowing users to configure their individual experience of the site by adding and removing modules from a 'home' page, subscribing to channels, and so on.

It's an impressive box of tricks, and one that non-web-based businesses of all kinds would do well to learn from – in terms, for instance, of providing value for customers by encouraging information-sharing, exchanges, comparisons and monitored feedback. It's an approach that takes some confidence, given that the essential dynamic of all five gaming techniques is not so much about fooling consumers into thinking that a product is 'fun' as about granting them a whole box of tools for making their own use of a product as powerful and convenient as possible. Above all, this means allowing people to interact meaningfully with each other and collectively to enhance the service they're receiving by giving out criticism as well as praise. Socially, as in the world of games, simple is rarely satisfying: what an environment like YouTube permits is emergent behaviours that have the space to take on a life of their own – and grant a commensurately complex satisfaction.

As far as human behaviour is concerned, one of the most intriguing opportunities video games offer is a unique combination of measurement and experiment. Literally everything within a game is measurable: every action, every interaction, every message, every item, every rule. The entire structure of a game is composed of raw, recordable data. Imagine, then, the kind of information that can be gathered by letting loose thousands, or hundreds of thousands, of human players within a carefully constructed virtual space.

Given that the membrane between working life and play is already more permeable than most people think, the opportunities for exploring human motivation, interests and habits are vast – and in no field is this more true than that of economics. Arguably the most important of all the social sciences, theoretical and practical debates in economics have a direct impact upon the lives of almost every person in some way. The vagaries of economics have repeatedly been exposed by the failures of the world's finest practitioners either to predict or to prevent most of the great financial disasters of the last few centuries – and, most recently, the global credit crisis that began in 2008.

Despite its empirical ambitions, economics is not an exact science – and is also one that seems fated to remain hostage to the more unpredictable depths of human behaviour. However, in the field of virtual worlds, and of video game studies in particular, there are those who believe that all this might be about to change. One such man, and a founding father of what is now known as virtual economics, is Edward Castronova, who since 2004 has worked as Associate Professor of Telecommunications at Indiana University. He began his career as an economics professor at California State University, but his interest turned increasingly towards the strange emerging phenomenon of virtual economies. Having gained his PhD in 1991 and spent some time studying the policies of German post-war reconstruction, as well as teaching in the subject areas of public policy and political science, he initiated the debate on virtual economics in earnest in 2001 when he published a paper entitled 'Virtual Worlds: A First-Hand Account of Market and Society on the Cyberian Frontier'.

The paper explored in considerable statistical detail the economy of 'a new world called Norrath, populated by an exotic but industrious people'. As its abstract observed, this Norrath presented a strange combination of the familiar and the entirely new:

> About 12,000 people call this place their permanent home, although some 60,000 are present there at any given time. The nominal hourly wage is about USD 3.42 per hour, and the labours of the people produce a GNP per capita somewhere between that of Russia and Bulgaria. A unit of Norrath's currency is traded on exchange markets at USD 0.0107, higher than the Yen and the Lira. The economy is characterized by extreme inequality, yet life there is quite attractive to many. The population is growing rapidly, swollen each day by hundreds of émigrés from various places around the globe, but especially the United States. Perhaps the most interesting thing about the new world is its location. Norrath is a virtual world that exists entirely on 40 computers in San Diego.

Here was perhaps the first detailed investigation into an astonishing scenario: tens of thousands of people pouring their time and energies into games whose strict conditions of scarcity, labour, reward and freedom of trading meant that a real and substantial monetary value could be placed on the monies generated by 'play' (in this case, the game was Sony's *EverQuest*). How seriously should or could all this be taken? Castronova put, and answered, the question on his very first page:

> Isn't Norrath just part of a silly game? Perhaps it is, on an abstract level. But economists believe that it is the practical actions of people, and not abstract arguments, that determine the social value of things. One does not study the labour market because work is holy and ethical; one does it because the conditions of work mean a great deal to a large number of ordinary people. By the same reasoning, economists and other social scientists will become more interested in Norrath and similar virtual worlds as they realize that such places have begun to mean a great deal to large numbers of ordinary people.

He then added, for good measure, an assessment of the potential of virtual worlds that is worth quoting in its entirety for its almost prophetic clarity:

> Virtual worlds may also be the future of e-commerce, and perhaps of the internet itself. The game designers who created thriving places like Norrath have unwittingly discovered a much more attractive way to use the internet: through an avatar. The avatar represents the user in the fantasy 3D world,

and avatars apparently come to occupy a special place in the hearts of their creators. The typical user devotes hundreds of hours (and hundreds of dollars, in some cases) to develop the avatar. These ordinary people, who seem to have become bored and frustrated by ordinary web commerce, engage energetically and enthusiastically in avatar-based on-line markets. Few people are willing to go web shopping for tires for their car, but hundreds of thousands are willing to go virtual shopping for shoes for their avatar.

Since 2001, the status of online game worlds has shifted by several orders of magnitude. At a conservative estimate, there are over 30 million people around the world with paid-for accounts in massively multiplayer games. Just in terms of legal revenue, the sector represents several billion dollars of annual income for the global industry and an unofficial market of virtual trade that's at least as large again. And yet, as Castronova sees it, these raw statistics are far from the most interesting thing about virtual economies. What's more amazing is just how much we may be able to learn from them about the real world within which they and we exist.

'The best way for any science to go forward,' Castronova explained to me when we spoke in March 2009, 'is for smart people to read literature, think deeply, theorize, and then try to create a controlled experiment to find out if their thinking is legitimate. In the natural sciences that is where we started in the seventeenth century. In social science, we don't do that. Only, now we can: we can create proper controlled experiments, we can use virtual worlds as Petri dishes.' What might this mean for economics in practical terms? 'You can get away from a lot of the ideology and theorising we're doing right now and become much more pragmatic about what is the right way to, for example, regulate a market that is very sparse in terms of its information, like the mortgage market. That sort of thing could be trivially easy to do controlled experiments on if we had a virtual world environment with, say, a hundred thousand people playing under the control of academics. It's not that hard to do.'

One key factor in this is just how far human behaviour in virtual worlds can be said to mirror human behaviour in the real world, and the first problematic word here is, once again, 'game', something that sounds a million miles away from the world of work and mortgages. Shouldn't any virtual world that hopes to model the real one even approximately stay as far away from the idea of play as possible? Absolutely not, argues Castronova. 'Fun first. What I say to a lot of professionals in the area is that you must surrender to the principles of a game. You have got to surrender to what the hairless monkey wants to do; and once you do that, you can do anything. I know people are suspicious of words like "fun". But I think you're not getting the whole person if you're compelling them.'

In other words, it's actually the structures of a successful game that make a virtual world – socially and economically speaking – a good model of the real one: the laborious, finely calibrated business of constructing and balancing aims, objectives, challenges and rewards. This isn't entirely surprising. When we think back to the reasons people play games in the first place, it's clear that the dynamics of a good game – of a truly satisfying one – are anything but trivial. When we are immersed in the flow of a game, Castronova notes, our behaviour is in many ways more natural and unaffected than at almost any other time, including during the routines of most kinds of work.

One area where the monitoring of in-game behaviour can be especially useful is the problem of market locations: the geographical question of where in a city, country or continent the optimum place to locate a trading hub lies. Trying to find such a spot is an extremely hard problem to solve mathematically; in scenarios approaching anything like real-world complexity in terms of landscape, people and paths, it's near-impossible. Yet modelling the same scenario within a game environment is both simple and largely faithful to real-life motivational and behavioural patterns: in each case, players will seek to minimise their effort and maximise their convenience. Thus, explains Castronova, 'there have been video games where the designers didn't specify where the player-to-player market would be, and its location has emerged according to very intuitive patterns; across different versions of the game it will tend to be in one of, say, three open, accessible, safe meeting places. It's all very intuitive and understandable in real world terms.'

On a more mundane level, a controlled study in 2008 of two parallel game worlds demonstrated a simple but crucial point: that players in virtual worlds appear to attach the same kind of importance to getting a good deal, and to striving to win value for their virtual money, as they do in real life; that is, they were prepared to pay twice as much for one item that was twice as effective as another. It sounds banal but, as Castronova points out, 'a lot of people think that if you go into a fantasy world you don't care about saving your pants any more. In fact you do, and we found a surprisingly robust confirmation of that behaviour.'

There's a surprisingly robust confirmation of something else to be found in games, too: the degree to which certain behaviours are deeply engrained in people. In the real world, scarcity is a fact of life. There isn't enough of everything to go around, and a lot of people suffer – or don't live as well as they might like to – as a result. You might assume, then, that given the opportunity to create a virtual world from scratch, scarcity would be one of the first things people would get rid of. Within a virtual world, after all, there can easily be enough of everything for everybody; where digital items are concerned it costs nothing to reproduce almost any object. Everything is just bits of data that can be copied at will.

The earliest virtual worlds were indeed lands of plenty. Places like *The Palace*, which opened its doors to the public in 1995, offered users a kind of enhanced chatroom where they could interact with each other within graphical environments ('palaces') that they had created themselves. Within the limitations of the technology, you could have and do anything you liked. It seemed like a fine template for the growth of other virtual environments – egalitarian places within which people could express themselves without any of the limitations real life imposed on them. Virtual utopias would rule.

What actually happened was rather different. People, it turned out, were extremely attached to scarcity. They liked it so much, in fact, that not only did they prefer virtual worlds in which there were strict limits on available resources over ones in which you could simply have anything you wanted; they were actually prepared to pay money to spend time in these scarce worlds. What they demanded, in other words, was a very particular kind of game: an environment where strict rules governed what it was possible for players to have and to do, and where, much as in the real world, rewards could only be achieved by the expenditure of effort. The principal difference with a game world being, of course, that within it effort was always rewarded.

The amount of effort people wanted to expend, too, proved quite staggering. Again and again, the most successful online games emerged as those that imposed brutal regimes of scarcity on their players. Even the non-elite majority seemed to enjoy watching other players strolling around wearing equipment that gave them the status of mythic heroes. Equality was dull. All players may have been created equal, but what they wanted was the opportunity to create, or to witness, a hierarchy.

From Castronova's perspective, this indicated that the time for setting theories and ideals above practical observations was long gone: it is no longer possible to pretend that you can change in some fundamental way what people are like or, indeed, what they like. 'It's like the discovery of a new continent,' he tells me. 'What we're developing here is a science of how to make people happy, and that's both a really exciting and a dangerous thing.

On the one hand it's exciting because we may be able to give people happy, fulfilled lives. But if we focus only on that we come into conflict with our understanding of what living a good life means. This is the notion that being hooked up to an experience machine that makes you happy all the time is not a good life, and we're going to have to confront this as a practical issue within a generation or two.'

Economics and hedonics, the study of human pleasure, are not the only two areas in which video games offer some pragmatic learning opportunities. One of the most famous case studies of mass behaviour within a game arose entirely by chance in *World of Warcraft* in September 2005, just a year after the game was launched. It began when a deadly disease generated by one especially tough monster (Hakkar, a blood god lodged at the heart of the Zul'Gurub dungeon) was accidentally transmitted by infected players to the world outside the confines of the dungeon. Within hours, the disease had become an epidemic. Known as the 'corrupted blood plague', tens of thousands of player characters succumbed. What was interesting, however, was not the pile of corpses itself, but the fact that the sequence of events during this entirely unscheduled incident bore more than a passing resemblance to a genuine pandemic outbreak within a human population.

It sounds a little absurd, especially as genuine death or injury are quite impossible within a video game, yet it attracted some very serious medical attention, including a paper in the American journal *Epidemiology*, by epidemiologist Ran D Balicer, which argued that 'virtual environments could serve as a platform for studying the dissemination of infectious diseases' and that they might prove 'a testing ground for novel interventions to control emerging communicable diseases'.

How could a virtual plague mirror a real one? For a start, it began in a remote area – an unexpected and isolated freak event, much like an isolated mutation in a virus such as avian influenza – and then spread via both humans and animals into population centres (in-game cities) where high densities of players quickly became hothouses for an uncontrollably escalating infection. There was also the known phenomenon of idle curiosity unwittingly contributing to the spread of the disease; and the existence of non-player-controlled characters who acted as 'carriers', spreading infection while themselves remaining healthy. Then, of course, there was the gamut of player reactions: experienced healing-class players offering their services in population centres to cure the diseased, guild leaders and those in positions of authority attempting to organise players and disseminate information, guild structures acting as support and information networks, many players hiding out in remote areas, not to mention engaging in all manner of speculation on the thousands of blogs and forums relating to *Warcraft*.

Why, though, did any of this matter? It was a question addressed at the Games For Health conference in Baltimore in 2008, when another epidemiologist, Nina H Fefferman, argued that the involvement of thousands of real people in games offered a way of modelling the unpredictable behaviour of humans in epidemic situations that no existing technique could match. The degree to which a game environment is able to model a real disease outbreak is, of course, limited. Yet it's the unreality of games that makes the modelling possible in the first place: there is simply no comparable 'real' method for studying the spread of a deadly disease in a population.

The ability to model virtual versions of extremely hazardous situations within games extends to areas other than health, of course. For instance, the deputy director of the US Center for Terrorism and Intelligence Studies (CETIS), Charles Blair, has pointed to the kind of tactics used by players within *World of Warcraft* (again, the world's most successful MMO is, perhaps inevitably, the one that attracts almost all the attention) who have dedicated themselves to causing maximum possible disruption to the game world by inflicting huge casualties on other innocent players. This kind of behaviour is a near-universal feature of popular multiplayer games: known as 'griefing,' it has evolved into a sophisticated sub-culture dedicated to the delights of ruining most people's fun in the most spectacular way possible. In the case of *Warcraft,* this has involved exploiting special features of high-end dungeons like the corrupted blood plague, which mischievous players then unleash like bombs in high-population areas to inflict maximum casualties. 'To put it academically,' Blair told *Wired* magazine, 'you have both dependent and independent variables' – that is, real people are making unexpected decisions within a controlled setting, giving a good indication of what approaches human ingenuity can come up with to try and get around rules and safety procedures designed to protect player populations.

Much of the pleasure that games offer comes from their combination of a sense of genuine achievement that nevertheless risks little that is 'real', and certainly not lives, health or even income. This is the source equally of their power and their limitations as models. As Castronova pointed out, you get to see some fundamental aspects of human motivation at work precisely because you are able to suspend certain other constraints.

The suspension of certain constraints within video games becomes most interesting when it is a question not just of mass behaviour, but of interpersonal behaviour – and the tools people have developed within games to better deal with each other and, in particular, with such problems as fairness and reward-sharing in complex group situations.

Consider one of the most fundamental problems posed by any online game: the distribution of rewards among a team of people who have collaborated in order to work their way through a particularly vast – and rewarding – challenge. Nobody is being paid to be there. In point of fact, as I noted in chapter 4, all the players involved will be paying exactly the same amount of money for the privilege of playing the game in the first place. Given that most in-game challenges tend to produce only a small amount of very valuable loot in the form of armour or weapons that almost everyone would like to own, the problem created is one that can only be solved satisfactorily by a solution that is self-evidently fair and self-contained.

In 1999 a group of players in the game *EverQuest* devised the first version of exactly such a system. Dubbed Dragon Kill

Points, or DKP (the key task that necessitated devising the system was killing two extremely tough dragons), essentially it entailed introducing a private and self-regulated currency between collaborating players. Under a DKP system, every time anyone participated in a group mission they got 'paid' a set DKP allocation. These points were tracked – usually on a website independent of the game, that all involved players have open access to – and accumulated over time until a player decided they wished to spend them on a rare or desirable item that had been found during an in-game mission. At this point, an open or closed auction system would allocate each item to the highest bidder.

Once the notion of DKP had been introduced (basically a binding, quantifiable social contract arranged between fellow players), an increasingly sophisticated series of methods of quantifying the challenges and rewards in the game soon began to develop among players. 'Price lists' were developed for in-game items, based on detailed statistical analyses of their properties. 'Zero sum' DKP systems were introduced, balancing out the number of points gained and spent during each raid in order to ensure the fairest possible distribution of loot over time. Then there were 'suicide' systems, with players ranked in a ladder of priority and those higher up having the right to get items ahead of those below them – at the price of committing 'suicide' and falling to the bottom; and so on. As one founder member of the *EverQuest* guilds that first developed the DKP system put it, 'loot handling in online games would probably be a PhD thesis in itself. It was very, very difficult. We had a good time trying to figure out what price things should be, what was the best way to distribute. We had to make and refine the rules as we went along, to keep people taking loot, spending their points rather than just saving them all up, while making sure the system was fair. I had to chase a few people out of the guild who just didn't get this.'

All this demonstrates the spontaneous emergence of cooperative human behaviour of the highest order in a setting where no obligation was placed upon players whatsoever to behave in this way. More importantly, though, there's the fact that, in an increasingly digital age, the field of gaming is a remarkably fertile one for creating better ways of working within and with digital media of all kinds. Above all, a DKP system maintains social cohesion among disparate people whose interests happen to coincide. It is an entirely self-enforcing mechanism; and yet, without any formal external framework or interventions, its success amongst gamers who adopt it runs at close to 100 per cent. This is largely because it works; it's transparent, meticulously fair, and has been laboriously calibrated over time in its various forms to prevent collusive bidding or other kinds of 'cheating'.

In the world of video games, inventions like the DKP system are small, sophisticated miracles with big implications. If you're looking to motivate a group of disparate people in a digital setting, this kind of internal value-setting is a hugely powerful mechanism; and it's a fine microcosm of what games can tell us about the value, thought and significance people attach to their actions in the supposedly anarchic, anonymous realm of remote communications and unreal consequences.

Precisely because they are not quite like the world, the study of video games can extract some extraordinarily powerful and useful lessons about what people are (or can be) like, and how best to motivate them. Can video games really bring certainty to the social sciences? Whatever transpires, they are in some sense already part of both the question and the answer. They have become a unique laboratory enabling us to study ourselves, and at the same time subtly shifting our sense of what it means to be a single self. If there's a lesson to be learned here, it's that many of the truths we're liable to discover through this kind of play are themselves likely to change us in the act of learning.

CHAPTER 10

Beyond fun

Video gaming may be an extremely serious business, and have the most serious of implications for the present century, but as soon as one starts sniffing around the burgeoning and contentious genre of 'serious games' themselves, the tension between what constitutes fun and what comprises a serious topic rises to the surface. No matter how much money a game makes or how great an impact it has, isn't there a troubling incompatibility here? Absolutely not, according to Suzanne Seggerman, the New York-based founder of the organisation Games for Change, a group founded in 2004 that promotes the use of video games as tools for raising political and social awareness.

As Seggerman sees it, 'fun' is an inadequate description of what video games do in the first place. 'I don't think the word is really right, I don't think a game has to be "fun". It has to be engaging, it has to be well-designed: what makes a game good is the balance of challenge and reward, and that is about learning.' At every step of a well designed game, you are engaged – but not necessarily entertained. It's a process she believes is fundamentally akin to some of the most serious issues in the world today. 'More and more we are recognizing in the twenty-first-century that the kind of problems we face globally are genuinely complex. They involve many interrelated variables: things relating to climate change or international trade, for example. Games are systems, and they offer a good way to explore complex systems, a way that we simply didn't have before.' There is, in other words, no better way to understand a complex system than by experiencing it: by role-playing, shifting variables, and seeing how the outcomes are affected.

This applies just as much to complex systems of conflicting human interests as to environmental or physical variables, as Seggerman explains. 'We gave out three prizes in 2006, not only to recognize what serious games are good, but also to help shape the field, which is still young. One of the three prizes was for raising awareness, and it went to a game called *Darfur is Dying*, which is available to play for free online. A lot of kids initially grabbed it because it had "dying" in the title, but it had a real impact.' In terms of 'impact', *Darfur is Dying* offers some impressive statistics. The game has been played by over three million people globally. It has also generated over 50,000 'actions', including letters to the US Congress. Those three million players come from a vastly broader – and younger – demographic than would usually be involved in such a complex political issue. This, of course, is another area where games come into their own: as a booming medium, they boast uniquely positive connotations and a long reach among a younger generation increasingly immune to the solicitations of print and television.

Playing *Darfur is Dying* couldn't be easier, so long as you have a computer and an internet connection. Visiting the game's website, you are instantly thrown into the fray: a window in the centre of your screen asks you to 'choose a Darfurian to represent your camp' from the eight members of a family presented in a hand-drawn line-up in front of you. This family of two parents and six children are your charges: displaced by conflict, the game asks you to perform such tasks as foraging for water, irrigating crops, and generally trying to survive the appalling rigours of life as one of the 2.5 million refugees in the Darfur region of Sudan (a context that's clearly explained in a couple of sentences underneath the game window onscreen).

I choose my family member, clicking on the image of Rahman, aged thirty, the father. Now I must forage for water – except I can't. A message has flashed up on the screen: 'It's very uncommon for an adult male to forage for water because he is likely to be killed by the Janjaweed militia. Choose another camp member to forage for water.' Right. Slightly nervously, I select the eldest child – Elham, a girl aged fourteen – for the task. I'm told to use the arrow keys to control Elham's movements, and then I'm off, dashing and dodging as the screen scrolls towards me. My mission is to dodge wandering militia by hiding behind rocks and scrub, and to reach the well, whose distance and direction in relation to me are indicated at the bottom of the screen.

It's tough. Incredibly tough, in fact. I can press the space bar to hide, but it isn't long before a jeep full of soldiers catches me out in the open. The screen freezes, and another blunt message flashes up: 'You have been captured by the militia. You will likely become one of the hundreds of thousands of people lost to this humanitarian crisis. Girls in Darfur face abuse, rape and kidnapping by the Janjaweed. As someone at a far-off computer, and not a child or adult in Sudan, would you like the chance to try again?' I would. One child down, five to go. I select the next eldest and set out once again into the scrub, dashing towards the well. This time, playing incredibly cautiously and hiding every hundred metres or so, I make it to the well. Success! I fill my canister and am promptly told I need to be extra careful as I'll now be moving much more slowly on my way back. Drawing a deep breath I set off for the camp, this time running towards rather than away from the screen – meaning I can't even identify any good hiding places in advance. A jeep appears in the distance, and I try to outrun it. Just a few hundred metres short of the camp, it catches me. I've lost another child and still not got any water.

At this point, several things occur to me. First, I'm not having much fun. I'm a pretty experienced gamer, and what I've been doing so far is both fairly crude and slightly excruciating. I'd like to get some water to the camp, but I have precisely nothing to show for my efforts; the loss of one more child might well push me over the I'm-never-playing-this-again edge. Second, I'm wondering whether my not having much fun is part of the point. After all, trying to get water to a real refugee camp in Darfur is neither fun nor easy, and the game may be honestly attempting to reflect this – which is both fair enough and somewhat self-defeating. It only takes a minute to absorb the lesson that getting water is a difficult task, and after this there isn't much to motivate me to continue in this task. As the game itself has already pointed out, I don't actually need this water because I'm sitting safe at home looking at a computer screen. What should keep me playing is a sense of challenge, achievement and engage-ment, and as yet I haven't found too much of that.

Still, there is more to the game than water-gathering. Or, to be more precise, there is more to this particular 'narrative based simu-lation' than water-gathering – the designers of *Darfur is Dying* were evidently sufficiently uneasy with the idea of referring to it as a 'game' that the word appears nowhere on their website that I can see. As well as gathering water, I can visit the camp itself, where I'm given an isometric overview of huts, fields and tents and tasked with assisting the residents in growing crops and main-taining the buildings. It's an attractively drawn setting, with plenty of mouse-over information about the details of life in such a camp; what it isn't, however, is either easy to fathom or to interact with. As I eventually work out, my job is to walk my character around the map, bringing water to and from a central supply in order to prevent the camp collapsing into chaos or starvation. Needless to say, the camp is regularly attacked and its facilities destroyed by militia. After eventually managing to make a successful water run, I manage to keep things going for only one day before it's game over. At which point a message asks me to enter my name, reminds me of the 2.5 million refugees currently living in camps, and invites me to spread awareness of the game virally to my friends. It also invites me to take further action by donating to charities working in Darfur, or contacting my elected representative.

Ethically, *Darfur is Dying* is hard to fault. It presents a great deal of important information with concision and impact. It's also attractively designed, well researched and has won a large audience for its message. As a game, however, its limitations are painfully obvious. It's a little confusing, extremely hard and largely unsatisfying in game-play terms. 'Fun' has been rather too scrupulously avoided; or, a little more generously, its idea of 'engagement' is somewhat dour and limited.

Seggerman herself admires the game, but is willing to concede that there's a significant divide in production values between most 'games for change' and the offerings of the mainstream industry. 'You can look at our organisation's website and you can truthfully say that these games do not yet stack up against the other kinds of games out there,' she admits. But she believes firmly that the idea of using video games as force for political and social engagement is one that will come into its own with time – and is extremely proud of what has already been achieved with titles like *Darfur is Dying*. 'This is such a new thing, it is only five years old. Like the film *An Inconvenient Truth*, there is going to be a game that really shows us what they can do, and changes the way people think. It is going to happen. I just hope it happens sooner rather than later.'

Part of the problem is money. *Darfur is Dying* was funded via a competition, backed by the American television channel mtvU, a division of MTV that broadcasts across the US to college students. Its design team was led by a talented student from the University of Southern California. All of which makes the finished product still more impressive as an achievement, but also highlights its limitations. Playing it is rather like going back in time fifteen years or twenty years, back to when most games were made on similarly small budgets under similar time constraints, and when players were less elaborately coddled by extensive play-testing, networked features and so on. There is tremendous enthusiasm for politically and ethically engaged gaming within much of the industry, but not – yet – the level of support from major developers and publishers that would be needed for the phenomenon to gain critical mass in terms of design and production values.

Beyond this, there remains the question of how far 'serious gaming' is a contradiction in terms. The idea that I might have been really entertained by *Darfur is Dying* is a somewhat uncomfortable one. Wouldn't the fact that I really enjoyed running a virtual refugee camp be, in some ways, inherently trivialising the issues involved? Seggerman rejects this idea, pointing to the impressive (and rapidly expanding) array of titles that her organisation is already linking to from their website, titles that model everything from Third World farming to spotting signs of addiction in others to developing sustainable energy resources for cities. 'Games have to be taken on their own terms,' she argues. 'They're not trying to replace the reality of Darfur or Rwanda. But people cannot just go and experience these places, and the simulated experiences games offer are amazing. I don't look on games as competing with the real world and human interactions. I see them as a medium and as a path towards actions in the real world.'

If you're looking for further evidence that games are serious tools for purposes other than entertainment, it can be found in a field whose aims appear very different to those of Games for Change – the military. Peter Singer details in his 2009 book *Wired for War* The US military alone now spends around $6 billion a year on various kinds of virtual and simulated training programs. Not all are video games in the strict sense, but the military were undoubtedly among the very first to realise the potential of games for both training and tactical development; and the brutal realities of their profession are such that there's little chance such an amount of money would be wasted on something that doesn't work.

War games themselves are almost as ancient as warfare; and many of the earliest games played in human societies were based around combat or fighting of some kind, from duelling and wrestling to javelin throwing. The earliest video games, too, found a rich resource for game designs in everything from hand-to-hand combat to virtual military campaigning. In fact, it's probably fairer to say that video games found the military, rather than the other way around.

The iconic first-person shooting game *Doom*, made by id Software, came out in 1993 and rapidly became one of the most successful titles of all time, not least because it was one of the first games to allow up to eight friends to link up their computers and chase each other around a landscape of bunkers, courtyards and hidden sniping points that they themselves could create customised maps for. In 1996, seeing how popular *Doom* was among soldiers, the US Marine Combat Development Command decided to produce a specially modified version of it.

Marine Doom, as it was inevitably known, was little more than a carefully reconfigured version of the existing game's run-around-a-maze-shooting dynamic. What it introduced was 'realistic' weaponry and a series of carefully structured environments, designed to train a team of marines in such disciplines as conservation of ammunition, the proper sequence of an attack and mutual support. It was also, not unimportantly, great fun. By modern standards the graphics were crude, but the experience was immediate, absorbing and nail-bitingly anxious, as well being notably effective at building the skills of communication and coordination necessary for a team to survive within it for any length of time.

As well as strategy and teamwork, hurtling around in-game environments proved a fantastic way of training soldiers to identify and memorise locations suitable for hiding, sniping, taking cover and regrouping, skills that were soon harnessed by the decision to construct training levels based on the precise floorplans of various worldwide US Embassies. This meant that, for example, hostage recovery scenarios could be rehearsed within accurate representations of actual Embassy buildings. As any gamer will tell you, there are few better ways of memorising the layout of a space than running around a virtual representation of it a few hundred times under intense pressure.

Marine Doom was a hit within the corps and, when a version of it was subsequently released for general consumption, outside it, a response which suggested a valuable secondary use for military video games, in parallel to their potential as training environments. They could also, the army realised, function as highly effective recruiting tools. What better way to harness the willingness of millions of gamers across the world to blow each other up in fantasy scenarios than to offer them a taste of the real thing – or, at least, to offer them a stamp of interactive military-grade authenticity? The result, released online in 2002, was the game *America's Army*, 'the official army game', as it bills itself on its slick website: simply download, create an account and you can start playing in a patriotic blaze of red, white and blue. Or rather, you can start training: *America's Army* isn't quite your standard blast-till-you-drop affair.

The first thing the game invites you to do is not – as some users might have hoped – kick some terrorist ass, but learn how to fire a gun in a training range, including full instructions on the importance of knowing how to unjam your rifle, conserve ammunition, and fire from standing, kneeling and prone positions. That done, it's on to an obstacle course – at which, during my first attempt, I manage to hurl myself to my death with an over-enthusiastic rope descent from a tower. The tone throughout isn't quite that of your ordinary gung ho game environment either: apart from paeans to the virtues of the American soldier on every loading screen, there's a strong emphasis on listening for and obeying orders, putting your safety and that of your comrades ahead of blasting or running around, and above all on maintaining what the game calls 'honour'. This is a kind of experience system that rewards players for 'honourable' actions, like aiding a comrade or achieving an objective, and punishes them for 'dishonourable' ones, like shooting civilians or allies. Fail to stick to the rules of each engagement and your soldier is likely to end up in prison.

America's Army, has been an unprecedented success, winning grudging respect even among the notoriously hard-to-please ranks of professional games journalists: a testament, among other things, to the money the military have invested in creating a product of commercial quality. At the time of writing, the PC version boasted 10,063,499 registered players (including this author). There have been no fewer than twenty-six editions of the game since its original release, spanning consoles as well as computers, and taking players through scenarios from special forces infiltrations to all-out assaults on terrorist bunkers or reconnaissance missions. It even holds the coveted Guinness World Records title of 'Most Downloaded War Game'.

Again, though, the basic tension between the idea of seriousness and the idea of entertainment rears its head. Is the triumph of *America's Army* as propaganda a tacit admission that the entire point of video games is the lack of certain kinds of real-world seriousness within them? You can certainly make the military seem a thrilling and thoroughly contemporary occupation by packaging it up in a hot new medium. Exactly how ethical an activity this is, however, remains open to debate. Indeed, as is often the way with modern video games, dissident voices have begun to be heard within the game itself, with a number of members of the public choosing to make 'virtual protests' against the actions of the US military by, among other things, registering accounts under the names of soldiers killed while on active duty in Iraq.

Think too long or hard about the ethical intricacies of a simulated environment modelling a combat situation and you're certain to experience a peculiarly modern kind of cognitive dissonance. It's something described in detail in reporter Evan Wright's

Generation Kill, an account published in 2004 of the author's experience of being 'embedded' with the First Recon unit of Marines on combat duty during the invasion of Iraq in 2003. The young men he watched fighting represented, he writes, 'more or less America's first generation of disposable children. More than half of the guys in the platoon come from broken homes and were raised by absentee, single, working parents. Many are on more intimate terms with video games, reality TV shows and Internet porn than they are with their own parents.'

Among other things, *Generation Kill* explores just how this tech-raised generation fared in a real battlefield. The answer is a mixed one. The men were deeply disturbed by aspects of their first encounters with real combat. It seemed that all the virtual violence in the world had, if anything, increased aspects of their essential innocence in the face of the mess and gore of real war. War is full of boredom, uncertainty and the visceral fear of death or terrible injury, none of which can really be modelled in even the most advanced virtual arenas. And yet the men Evan Wright described were also fine soldiers: brave, highly competent, and possessed of an almost total mastery of the often bewilderingly complex technologies at their disposal.

In this respect, it's clear that being well prepared for modern warfare shares many elements with good preparation for modern life: you need to be able to live and breathe certain kinds of software and hardware. Most of your actions are mediated by complex machines, while your sphere of power and information extends well beyond the personal space you occupy. You are a networked individual, using multiple tools, often deluged with information and options. In the case of war, senior commanders today have a bewildering arsenal of options at their disposal, and often only extremely limited amounts of time to make decisions. These men and women may not be in a game; but nor are their actions in any sense unmediated. In other words, anyone hoping, or fearing, that someone can be psychologically prepared for the consequences of combat by playing a game is likely to be disappointed. But anyone who thinks that games fail to offer soldiers any experiences truly relevant to their most serious purposes has failed to think sufficiently about what 'relevant' really means today.

Military games, in this respect, are not so dissimilar from many 'games for change.' What a game can do, as Suzanne Seggerman noted, is turn just about any complex and potentially overwhelming system of variables into a manageable simulation that can be played, refined and analysed as many times as you want. It's a process that, compared to the cost and hazards of 'real' training exercises, offers fantastic value for money. And, most intriguingly of all, it overlaps directly with one of the most potent and rapidly developing fields not just of modern warfare, but of all kinds of human exploration, excavation and interaction with the most hazardous and challenging of environments – robotics.

Unmanned aircraft have been in use for reconnaissance purposes by both the British and American military since the 1960s. Today, however, technology has advanced to the point where highly complex remote-controlled 'drone' aircraft, known rather chillingly as Reapers, are being used for everything from interception and exploration missions to true 'hunter killer' roles. The operation of these machines bears more than a passing resemblance to a certain electronic leisure pursuit. In simple terms, drone aircraft – of which the US military alone now operates more than 7,000 – are designed for complete integration with both video game simulations and video game control mechanisms. It can be literally impossible to tell apart a training scenario, taking place via a 'virtual' drone within an environment generated by a modified version of the *America's Army* game, from an actual mission as relayed by the multiple cameras and sensors attached to a real drone. Moreover, with every aspect of the control system in the training and real scenarios being identical, simulated interactions can be switched to 'live' ones at the flick of a switch. As a profile in *Wired* magazine revealed, America's top drone pilot is not a swaggering *Top Gun* type, but a high-school dropout whose great aptitude was not for action but for video games.

Similarly, the increasing use of 'remote-controlled-soldiers' – caterpillar-track mounted robots able to wield machine guns, travel through snow, sand and water and relay home detailed images from their onboard cameras – blurs the line between simulation and reality in a disturbing, if highly effective, manner. Again, by using a specially adapted module and control system from the *America's Army* game, soldiers can employ exactly the same controls and video interface to engage in both virtual and actual combat situations. Thus far, the main use of the robots has been for tasks like mine-clearing (units performed over 20,000 bomb disposal missions in Afghanistan and Iraq) but other engagements are only a matter of time, as is the inevitable escalation of the hardware and software involved.

The possibility of robot armies marching across the world under the control of youths wielding video game controllers within sealed military bunkers is a frightening one (not least because this kind of thing can sound dangerously attractive to certain kinds of gaming ears); and yet, rather more hopefully, it's in areas other than shooting that the wider possibilities of the kind of games the military have invested so much money in really start to become obvious, and to get closer to what are perhaps the most essential 'serious' capacities of video games. Take, for example, a 'virtual training program' video game that has been developed for US military officers. Known as *Gator Six*, and based on hundreds of actual combat situations, the game uses actors and location filming to put players into the kind of decision-making situations that young officers actually face in the field. Short segments of video are played, a voiceover explains the key facts of each situation, and then you're left to select actions from a number of multiple choices that gradually draw you deeper into each unfolding scenario.

A demonstration version of the software throws players in at the deep end with a video outlining a scenario similar to that faced by many units in Iraq. Combat operations within a fictional nation have just come to an end, and it's your task as a young captain to pacify a town by maintaining order there and preparing it for a peaceful transition to democracy. With just ninety-five soldiers at my disposal and an irascible colonel breathing down my neck, I began the campaign with two options: did I want to 'get the lay of the land' by taking things slowly and staying outside the town for a day, or 'roll through heavy to signal that you're in charge'. I went for 'heavy', and was soon in a meeting with a local leader trying to assert my influence. How to behave towards this prickly power-broker: make bold promises, 'maintain cultural distance' or 'lessen expectations'? I decided to stick ruthlessly to the mission imparted by my colonel: stop any insurgency in its tracks, stop the looting, don't show weakness.

Soon, I was enjoying my second drive-by shooting in twenty-four hours. I decided to lay an ambush, and shoot to kill. And so on. Ten or so decisions later, my inexperience was laid bare as my men suffered heavy casualties under the combined weight of an ambush, mortar fire and a still-hostile local population's contributions. A final video played, spelling out exactly how the decisions I made compounded to bring disaster. I listened to my men dying over the radio. It certainly made an impression.

Gator Six, which is produced for the military by the specialist serious games design company WILL Interactive Inc., is memorable and impressive – and the non-military applications of its set-up are easy enough to imagine. Indeed, WILL Interactive themselves boast a range of training titles that deal with everything from suicide prevention to, in the case of the aptly titled *Anatomy of Care*, helping a hospital handle poor customer satisfaction. The company describes its products as 'slice-of-life experiential learning programs', and has a patent for the 'interactive behaviour modification process' that allows them to generate behaviours sophisticated enough to be useful.

Yet even the most complex video-and-multiple-choice game looks crude in some ways in comparison to the kinds of training simulations based on games technology that are already being piloted in other professions. Medicine is one area in which the use of game and virtual techniques is especially advanced – perhaps partly because the business of caring for the human body involves understanding the real-time interactions of countless complex systems and games are especially powerful at reproducing such systems.

One vital area of training is emergency triage: equipping healthcare professionals to assess the order in which casualties should be seen in a crisis situation. The principles apply equally to events like train crashes, treating sick people in remote areas, or even military operations; the underlying idea is that it's vital, when time and resources are limited and needs are devastatingly urgent, to differentiate between those patients who might be saved by intervention and those who won't be.

Take the example of the 'wilderness' training many British doctors undergo at conferences and on training courses in Scotland. Typically a climbing accident is simulated: a number of volunteers lie down at the bottom of a small cliff; next to each victim stands an instructor, who will answer questions put by the trainee about the condition of each victim – their pulse, blood pressure, wounds, responsiveness. There are also a number of printed cards explaining the bare bones of the scenario. Such exercises usually involve around ten instructors and serve perhaps a couple of dozen students. They are, in other words, extremely resource-intensive; and, while they are expertly run and scrupulous in the medical details, they also offer only a minimal degree of realism and interaction.

Compare this set-up to a prototype triage game currently under development by the TruSim division of Blitz Games Studios, whose areas of research include serious gaming. In the triage game, everything takes place in an interactive three-dimensional world: you explore the site of, for example, an explosion in a city, and find the bodies of those who need treatment as you investigate the wreckage. With highly realistic graphics and an interface that allows users to monitor vital signs, the data presented mirrors almost everything a medic would be able to discover about these patients in a real-life situation and, crucially, forces them to take triage decisions in real time without any break in the immersion.

The game is much less mediated than the 'real' scenario; and, of course, the cost of running dozens or even hundreds of such game situations is negligible. 'It's interesting,' one doctor who had watched the TruSim demonstration told me, 'because how can you simulate a complex, open fracture of the leg in real life? You can't, at least not without a lot of tomato ketchup. But in a game, you can represent difficult wounds exactly. For large-scale emergency training, at the moment, they have people dressed up in latex and fake blood, pretending to be in a car crash. It's involving, but it's also very obviously unreal. A virtual world can simulate the noise, the chaos, everything. You could assess, for example, the exact percentage and degree of someone's burns from the way they looked in a game.' And, of course, you could roll out such a scheme across the country and compare data and different approaches between centres at a minimal cost: game technologies excel at nothing so much as scoring, comparing and rewarding progress (medics, moreover, are a notoriously competitive bunch in the first place).

Perhaps the most important single demonstration of the potential of games for serious applications comes not from combat or emergency medicine but the purest of all training environments: the education system. There will inevitably come a time when no one alive remembers a time before video games existed. Like books and movies, they will be a part of the media landscape older than living memory. Within a modern school, that time has already arrived: every single pupil was born into a world where video games were simply a fact of life, and it's in this environment and among these pupils that the serious potential of video games suddenly starts to seem less a novel possibility than a creeping inevitability – as much a fixture in our future lives as the mobile telephone or the computer screen.

Until 1999, Derek Robertson was a primary school teacher in Scotland. 'I still am at heart,' he says, when we first speak in March 2009, although his official job title has moved on considerably since those days. From 2001 to 2006, he lectured on the postgraduate course in primary teaching at Dundee University;

from August 2006 until June 2008 he was a development officer seconded to an organisation known as Learning and Teaching Scotland; and since then, he has boasted the title of National Adviser for Emerging Technologies and Learning in Scotland. It's largely thanks to him that Scotland now leads the world in the emerging field of what Robertson calls 'games-based learning'.

Even a decade ago, Robertson was profoundly sceptical of everything to do with video games. Then, in 1997, on the last day of term before Christmas, the children got to bring in toys and games, one of which happened to be a Super Nintendo games console. 'I watched these two boys play a game,' he explained, 'where they were manipulating and arranging 2D shapes forming sequences and patterns. They were doing this really quickly, but what interested me was that these boys were in my supposedly bottom maths set and, when it came to problem solving in the traditional contexts with which I was presenting them, they appeared to be pretty hopeless. But this game challenged my thinking. How come they were so good at problem solving in the context I was watching, via a computer game?'

So Robertson began trying out games in the classroom, according to what he felt were the principles of best practice in teaching: involvement, engagement, stimulation and rigour. He used, for instance, Nintendo's series of *Zelda* adventure games to get children to write stories known as 'ergodic' texts – that is, stories with no single linear path, where a reader's decisions about which page to turn to next give rise to a whole range of narratives. It was an instant success, as was the learning of various mathematical principles through other games. Yet the key point was not that video games achieved miraculous results but that, as he put it to me, they were a context that really meant something to the children. 'I think it's very important that learning doesn't look at a child as though they come out of a vacuum: that school embraces where children come from and what there is out there that impacts on their cultural life.' Within the digital culture that all children are now born into, of course, video games have tremendously positive connotations, and, given that their most basic mechanisms are in many ways simply variations on the common theme of learning, it was probably only a matter of time before they began to find their way into educational structures.

Robertson's great opportunity came during his initial secondment to Learning and Teaching Scotland, when, with the small budget he was given, he decided to create a physical space where he could bring all kinds of people – education managers, pupils, teachers – to get their hands on the actual games and discover that 'it wasn't all *Pac-Man, Space Invaders* and blowing up zombies'. He dubbed this space the 'Consolarium', and began to take it on tour. His mission was, in a sense, twofold: to take on people's initial misconceptions about what video games actually were; and to change their perception of how games might be used within schools. Games, he emphasised, were not magical learning mechanisms designed to take the place of teachers. They were, rather, a powerful new tool able, in the hands of a good teacher, to 'engage the most uninterested of pupils as well as challenge the best'.

It's a field in which the results have begun to speak for themselves. In 2008, the year Robertson was invited to take on his official role as Scotland's National Adviser for Emerging Technologies and Learning, he oversaw the most extensive trial to date of what games-based learning might mean for schools. Extended across thirty-two Scottish schools and involving over 600 pupils, the study was conducted to the most rigorously controlled scientific standards. First, every pupil involved at every school took an initial maths test, and their scores were recorded. They were then split into two groups, with sixteen schools in each. The trial group used, under structured supervision, a game on the Nintendo handheld DS console – *Dr Kawashima's Brain Training*, which contains a number of mental arithmetic training games – for twenty minutes at the start of every day for nine weeks. The control group simply continued their classes as normal. At the end of the nine weeks everyone was tested again. Both groups had improved, but those using the game had shown a 50 per cent greater improvement than those who had not. The time the games group took to complete the test had also dropped by more than twice that of the control group.

Equally significantly, the increases in the game group were most significant among pupils at the lower end of the ability spectrum. It's a suggestive, and hugely impressive, set of results on a number of levels. But the most important single issue is, Robertson believes, one of attitude. 'We find some pupils are disengaged from learning by the traditional fear they get from school. And the games are really powerful at dealing with this, at enthusing people, not so much in themselves as via the context for learning that the teacher manages to craft around them.' I asked how many schools are now using video games in learning across Scotland? 'I would say at least two hundred. I've given local authorities the kit to get them started as well as loaning it out, and I go out taking the Consolarium on tour, giving talks, bringing it all with me. And it has really kicked off now. Attitudes have transformed since I started in 2006. If you come to Scotland, you will see the computer game being treated as a valid learning tool: with teachers, by teachers, for teachers. We have repositioned games-based learning from being a left-field idea to something that is very much main-stream.' Such has been his success that games-based learning has now even been listed in the new Scottish national curriculum documents.

In terms of the all-important 'contexts from learning', it's not all maths games, of course. One of the most impressive examples Robertson gives of a games-based learning experience involves his use of the *Guitar Hero* games, and allows pupils to play along with their most beloved rock idols.

The games themselves are tremendous fun but not, outside of the musical skills of timing and listening, what you might think of as especially educational. What Robertson has done with them, however, is to use a relatively short amount of time spent actually playing the game as a 'contextual hub' around which other curricular activities are driven. Why has he taken such an approach; and why use a video game rather than, say, a real guitar or a CD? 'Because, if there's one thing I've learned, it's that learning through a context is powerful. And with a game

203

like *Guitar Hero*, the children can let themselves go, forget they're in school, forget there is some degree of image involved. And then they can, all of them, really start learning.'

In practice, this involves a term's worth of detailed scenario and context-building. 'The teacher who was organising this first got the children to write a biography of an imaginary rock star, after looking at examples. Then they looked at each other's writing and got the best five into a virtual band for the class. The band then made an album. Then – with all this plot coming from the children – it was decided that the album had gone double platinum, and the band had to go on a European tour. And this meant that they had to plan an itinerary, research capital cities and transport routes across Europe, hotel costs, flights, times, currencies. In design and technology they made guitars out of card, paper and string; and then hung these up and created a guitar shop. Then they had to create a video for an awards ceremony.'

The list of tasks goes on. It's an incredible, and somewhat overwhelming, itinerary. But did it work? 'Absolutely,' he tells me. 'We now have places like East Lothian council using this as a transition project between primary and secondary schools: so primary pupils in their final term before they move to secondary school all do a *Guitar Hero* project, and then go for a "rock day" to their new secondary school and meet their classmates and take part in lots of activities.' In fact, they even now have a national *Guitar Hero* challenge taking place in Scottish schools, with a national leaderboard operating on another jewel in the crown of Scottish learning, a dedicated high-speed broadband network for schools known as Glow. 'I had parents and pupils send in their high scores last year,' Robertson tells me. 'And the top four went to Glasgow for our learning festival, and there was a stage, a PA and lights, and a prize. And this year we now have teams of pupils competing.'

Robertson's passionate enthusiasm is infectious – and in Scotland schools, parents, local authorities and councils are now queueing up to participate in the latest wave of video games learning. Elsewhere, many Asian countries also take game-based learning seriously. Nintendo's consoles and brain-training games were born in Japan, where their popularity dwarfs that found in any other country, and where educational titles are increasingly being used to keep the minds of the elderly population sharp as well as engaging youthful ones. It's Scotland, however, that is for the time being the global cutting edge; and one country reaping the benefits of proximity is England, with initiatives based on Robertson's work starting to spring up at a number of centres around the country.

One such centre is Oakdale Junior School in Essex. Game-based learning came to Oakdale after the borough heard Derek Robertson speaking about his work in early 2008. Like many others before them, the local education authority were so impressed by Robertson's work and results that they bought thirty Nintendo DS consoles and invited all secondary and primary schools in the area to bid for them. Oakdale was one of the first schools to get their hands on the consoles and have for the last year been running their own trial version of

Robertson's scheme, under the aegis of form teacher Dawn Hallybone.

As in Robertson's initial Scottish tests, the main game used is *Dr Kawashima*: a typical class, packed with thirty pupils aged ten and eleven, was buzzing with quiet activity soon after Hallybone gave out the Nintendo handheld consoles, with pupils striving to beat each other – and her – at twenty mental arithmetic questions. After a few attempts, she called play to a halt and asked pupils to recall the 'tricks' and techniques they had been learning to help them master mental maths: times tables, how to break big numbers down into smaller ones, how to deal with zeroes, fives and tens, and so on. Hands shot up eagerly and note was furiously taken of everything that would help them do the sums faster.

The pupils loved the competition because the machines kept score instantly and automatically, and were scrupulously fair; everyone could do a test at the same time and then compare results. They loved the presentation and interface ('you get to see one sum ahead, and it scrolls so smoothly,' one girl commented), perhaps unsurprisingly, given that several billion dollars' worth of corporate research and development have gone into making the consoles as child-friendly as possible. They loved the touch screens, the neat snappy cases, the visual and verbal rewards every time they got something right. Although, one ten-year-old boy explained with an extremely serious look on his face, 'I'd like to do more games in schools, but I think it's not like a good idea to be on this all the time. In the future I will play games, but it won't be like an hour and a half a day, I won't be mad.' There were also, a girl sitting next to him added, benefits beyond maths skills to be gained: 'I have this world records book, and it says that games improve your eyesight if there's a tiny thing and you're trying to aim at it.'

During this class and several others, a central point about game-based learning gradually became obvious. For teachers and parents, using games consoles as part of a lesson may still sound a little like science fiction, or at least like gimmickry. For pupils like those at Oakdale, however – a good local state school representing a whole spectrum of abilities, ethnicities and attitudes – the presence of the consoles in the classroom was a natural and familiar extension of much else in their lives. As pupil after pupil patiently noted, this was a welcome slice of their 'real' lives transplanted into the sometimes-daunting world of the classroom. With this kind of technology in their hands, even the weakest member of the class felt entirely at home. So at home, in fact, that they competed to come back in break times to take more maths tests.

Oakdale's head teacher, Linda Snow, is philosophical on this point. Had parents been cynical, even hostile, to the idea of her school using video games as a learning method? 'No one has complained, quite the reverse. I know my husband, who is a head at another school, has had parents asking why they aren't doing this too. There has been a lot of competition to have the machines.' And what about the pupils? 'Children now see everything in fifteen-second bursts. Gone are the days when they sat for thirty minutes copying off a board: they expect the world to be singing and dancing. Dawn uses Twitter live in her class, live links with Australia for geography, posting stuff on websites: this is a world that even five years ago wasn't there. And the DS consoles are part of that package. For the pupils, it's not like, gosh, this is something new. They grow up with this technology. It's part of who they are, now.'

CHAPTER 11

Future Inc.?

Here is one prediction for the future that can't be repeated too often: people won't change. What they do, how they do it and who they do it with will change, but if there's one lesson that video games in particular should remind us of, it's that the most powerful aspects of our natures are both very ancient and very hard to alter.

What video games do, like most technology, is amplify particular human tendencies: our innate hunger for learning, our delight in solving problems and challenges, our sociability and rivalries, our pleasure in escaping the uncertainties of the world for more predictable rewards. Then, too, there are the ways in which games as interactive systems increasingly connect to the ways in which we work, communicate, plan and express ourselves in a digital age, a process that is making the world more playful, and where the business of play is becoming ever broader and more profitable. The very term 'video game', although it is likely to linger for historical reasons, will increasingly be stretched by the multiplying sub-genres and expanding boundaries of all that it encompasses.

When it comes to specifics, predicting the future of a medium whose defining characteristics are the disruption of established business models, regular transformative innovations and an increasing proliferation of sectors is almost impossible. Yet the coming years, and even decades, do hold at least a few near-certainties. For a start, there's the demographic observation that the world now hosts its very first generation of 'digital natives' – a slightly sinister pseudo-anthropological description of those born into the age of the internet, the mobile phone, the laptop and the console. Over the next half-century, video games are going to become as much a part of everyone's daily experience as television, radio, automobiles, refrigerators, type and the written word; and this means their audience is going to go on growing for many years yet, and will continue to mature and divide into genres for all ages and situations. 'Grandma gaming' is a joke phrase today; tomorrow, it could be one of the most profitable sectors around.

Another certainty is money – lots of money. From its current value at $42 billion and double-digit annual growth rate, there's no reason to suppose that the video games industry will stop at the $50 billion or even the $100 billion mark. Video games already possess both successful and robust models for making money from their users, online and offline; and the kind of service that virtual worlds can offer is likely to remain at a premium for years to come, even if it shifts towards funding via advertising and micro-payments rather than the subscription model currently dominant in the West.

Apart from shared virtual worlds, one other sector with huge growth potential is the somewhat ill-defined area known as casual games: short, sweet, low-commitment doses of high engagement delivered to everyone from busy working bosses on commuter trains to pensioners waiting for their hair to set. With mobile computing platforms only just beginning to show what they're capable of, this kind of rapid on-demand fun may well offer a more accurate image of the 'gaming' of everyday life than that of high-commitment virtual worlds, where immersion and effort put severe limits on when and how people are able to play. So far as technology is concerned, convenience and instant satisfaction have a far broader potential for growth than highly sophisticated, demanding products that on paper appear far more impressive.

Then there are alternative interfaces, which have just started to come into their own thanks to the latest generation of mass-market advances by console manufacturers. We are entering an age of neurological control, facial and postural recognition, and real-time sensory feedback – one where remote human interactions will increasingly involve more than simply sounds and images, and where three-dimensional displays will finally start to become a realistic option for home users. We can expect games to remain at the forefront of this field, with physical feedback and motion detection as standard in every gaming device in the near future. Away from the home, location-based gaming will also offer a different kind of interaction, with GPS-enabled gamers tying up with everything from Google maps to TripAdvisor.

Contrary to the old-fashioned vision of video games as isolating experiences, it's social interactions of various kinds that are – and will continue to be – the biggest single engine driving both gaming and modern media progress as a whole. Facebook overwhelmingly dominates this field, but it is games and the increasing 'gamification' of online social activities that represent perhaps the most important trend in this field. Certainly, from a business perspective, it's social and casual games that are creating many of the most powerful models for profiting from the kind of casually intermingled social and playful activities that increasingly constitute the daily texture of digital experience. There are risks here of both exploitation and – perhaps more importantly in the long run – boredom and frustration on the part of users, whose tastes tend to evolve several times faster than the development cycles of most companies.

Still, the casually 'gamed' arenas of social networks are one of the most important and rapidly developing of all contemporary digital spaces.

On the hardware side of things, mobile internet technology is the undisputed key to the immediate future. First-generation mobile phones were terrible gaming platforms: they offered no business model whatsoever to developers or publishers, and no marketplace to speak of for customers wishing to purchase games of a decent quality. All this has now changed beyond measure. Every year, approximately as many mobile phones are sold as home computers have ever been sold. As of the last few years, these phones are increasingly able to function as internet-enabled computers in their own right – and this, complete with the capacity for customers to purchase and install independently developed applications on them, represents a global technology revolution all of its own.

The iPhone is by far the most successful example of this kind of device, thanks to its aesthetic appeal, slick interface and the masterful precision of its online marketplace for downloadable software, the App Store. And here the statistics already speak for themselves. During the first year of the Apple App Store's existence, between July 2008 and July 2009, over 1.5 billion applications were downloaded. This is just a marketplace for Apple products to be used on Apple phones, yet it's already worth over $1 million a day in revenues. And, in obedience to one of the most reliable long-term principles of any programmable technology platform, the one thing people seem to want to do on their iPhones more than anything else (apart, perhaps, from phoning people) is to play games.

The single most popular and populous set of applications on the App Store are games. In July 2009, 'Games' and 'Entertainment' (programs that are essentially mini-games or puzzles) were the No.1 and No.2 categories of App respectively, with 10,805 active Games (18 per cent of the total) and 8,508 Entertainment programs (14 per cent). There were also another 3,900 (6.5 per cent) classified as Education titles, most of which are simply serious games that teach maths, languages and so on. These three areas together account for almost 40 per cent of all iPhone applications – and some of them are rather good. The No.1 paid-for download in July 2009 was, as you might expect, a video game (so were No.2 and No.3). In *I Dig It*, which costs just a couple of dollars, you play a farmer who's obliged to burrow away through the earth underneath his farmhouse in a specially adapted digger in order to uncover rare metals, minerals and so on. He has to do this, you're told, in order to pay the mortgage on the farm: a pleasingly unlikely combination of credit crunch concerns and science fiction solutions. With beautifully hand-drawn graphics and an intuitive touch-screen control method, it's cheap, quirky fun of the kind that's increasingly dominating the free time of much of the Western world.

With 45 million iPhones sold already, it's conceivable that the iPhone could, on its own, become the world's most important gaming platform within a few years. What's certain is that Apple's App Store – and its policy of allowing developers to submit their applications for approval and sale within the Store cheaply and easily – has established a model that will be emulated everywhere by pretty much anyone who wants to make a success of their own mobile internet phones and future technology platforms – all of which, of course, are likely to boast games as their top-selling software draws. The gaming revolution hasn't just left the bedroom and entered the living room: it's out on the streets, in people's pockets and amusing them on trains as they come home from work.

Despite all this potential for growth and influence, there still remains an element of paradox in the modern video games industry: a result, in part, of the enormous momentum older models of media production still have. As far as most individual companies are concerned, making and selling traditional, big-budget video games remains a deeply uncertain commercial proposition. This perception is shared to some degree with all the creative industries. Creating a hit is an art, not a science. Big games are extraordinarily complex products that demand substantial up-front investment, and this means that many established games publishers are likely to remain conservative in their outlook, relying on established brands and series for the bulk of their income. Smaller companies, meanwhile, may be able to make a splash with digitally distributed delights, but they face an uphill struggle to break into the realm of serious profit. Much of the money is still in boxed product, old-fashioned distribution and online extras to keep players happy.

While the current generation of consoles remain on the market – the PlayStation III, the Xbox 360, the Nintendo Wii – this is unlikely to change. Too much money has been spent by their manufacturers in developing them, and by publishers and developers in learning how to develop games for them. Yet this generation of consoles may well be the last time that the gaming industry sees what has been, for the last two decades, a constant cycle of vast initial expenditure on developing new hardware, translating after a few years into huge profits, thanks to licensed software sales on the several hundred million hardware units that have been sold.

Nicholas Lovell, an industry analyst who has spent the last fifteen years working and advising companies in the overlapping areas of technology, media and finance, is one man who believes that the present generation of games consoles may also be the last. 'I believe the console is dead and the future is online,' he argues. 'The current generation of consoles is predicated on companies subsidizing a very expensive piece of hardware, and recovering their money mainly through a tax on everyone who wants to develop games for their platform. You can make some money selling consoles at the end of their life-cycle, after all the research and development is paid off, but the core of the model is that the console manufacturers have absolute control over their platforms and over who gets to develop games for them.'

The old model, in other words, relies on everyone wanting to develop games for Sony, Microsoft and Nintendo's machines – and being willing to pay a hefty premium to do so. And this, Lovell believes, is a situation that in the age of an open internet is no longer sustainable. 'Anyone at all can develop games for the PC, for websites in general, and for devices like the iPhone. And what that means is that the game the console manufacturers are fighting is the same old battle that other companies fought at the start of the internet, of a walled garden over open access. In the end, in my opinion, it is inevitable that the open world will kill the closed one.'

It's an analysis that is, in many ways, music to the ears of the business community. Accel Group is one of the largest global venture capital firms to specialise in interactive media. Founded twenty-five years ago in Silicon Valley, it has since expanded across America, Europe, China and India, and now manages a pool of over $6 billion in investment. Yet only recently has it decided that the video games industry is ripe for the kind of investment it has historically put into companies such as Facebook, BitTorrent, Real, Macromedia, comScore and numerous other blue-chip internet players. As one of their senior partners, Simon Levene, who joined the company in 2006 and has a particular interest in internet-based services and entertainment software, explained: 'Gaming, historically, is really not an area that has attracted a lot of professional venture capital. And this is because it really has been a hits-driven business – and because the economics have really been stacked against development studios, what with the power of a few publishers controlling distribution and the required amount of capital and time needed to build really good games just growing and growing.'

The situation for those investing in internet-based games today looks very different. Cost of entry is lower. Time to build is much shorter. Time to market is much faster. And the cost of failure is far less devastating. Moreover, distribution is no longer reliant on the cooperation of a publisher with heft in big retail outlets: titles can be bought online from anywhere, and success can spread as much by word of mouth and online friendships and social networks as by expensive advertising campaigns. 'All of this,' Levene explained, 'makes it a very different industry to the one we shied away from twenty years ago. If you look at the statistics from people like ComScore, they think that between 5 and 10 per cent of all time spent online is spent playing games. And that doesn't even include people playing things like *World of Warcraft* via specialised clients rather than in browsers. It is an unbelievable amount of human time, billions of hours, and it is growing far faster than the rest of the web.'

However; console manufacturers are not simply going to sit back and watch their business model die. For a start, there's the example of the Nintendo Wii, which by refusing even to compete with the raw processing power of Sony's and Microsoft's machines introduced a hugely successful new model into a marketplace hitherto dominated by raw processing power: a fun-led, lower-powered platform, with the emphasis firmly on appealing to consumers by innovation and entertainment value rather than graphical and sonic marvels.

Beyond this, though, lies a still more important point, at least as far as Sony and Microsoft are concerned: the fact that the real battle heating up in living rooms around the world is not so much about being the world's video gaming machine of choice as about being the world's all-singing, all-dancing media box. This is why Microsoft entered the console war in 2001 in the first place: because it realised that the market for electronic play was about to blossom into something far bigger. With all consoles now boasting wired and wireless internet capacities, and the ability to play DVDs, audio CDs and other media with ease (although only Sony's PlayStation III can so far boast a Blu-ray player), they are increasingly positioning themselves not just as games machines, but as media hubs, able to offer everything from on-demand television and movie services to media playing and social networking. Microsoft has proved itself the nimblest of the big players here, and has already announced a live television service in partnership with Rupert Murdoch's BSkyB in the UK. This will effectively provide a satellite television service via a console through a broadband connection rather than a dish; and it will compete directly with the set-top boxes that – complete with the ability to record and manage television programmes digitally on a hard disk – are now the mainstay of the pay-television industry.

Given the number of consoles in use around the world – which, including handheld machines, is already close to half a billion – the idea of exclusive console-based television content is likely to prove an extremely appealing one for both struggling television companies and their equally audience-hungry advertisers. And given the hardware and software sophistication of most consoles, as compared to most cable and recordable television boxes, the battle to deliver a top quality product is one consoles are in a strong position to win, should they choose to fight it.

In fact, with consumers' expectations of all media increasingly tending towards the interactive – recordable digital television, music that is purchased and managed as discrete MP3 files, photographs that exist and are displayed only on screens – gaming machines are remarkably well placed to become the single indispensable object sitting next to any flat-screen television. They are operating in a different league to PCs in terms of design, interfaces and sheer consumer cool: PCs for browser-based fun; consoles for living room media; smartphones for everything else. The future is looking increasingly like a triple-platform place – with everything socially linked and synchronised online, and the games software industry cropping up everywhere and anywhere there's a media product being consumed. It won't be long before the first games are released for e-book readers like Amazon's Kindle: the idea of any media platform in possession of a market-place lacking games seems unlikely to last for long.

In fact, perhaps the most significant challenge to the console model of gaming is not so much competition from PCs as the more radical possibility of removing most of the hardware from the homes of individual consumers entirely. Much like 'cloud computing', where the remote use of powerful central computers via the internet is already revolutionising many people's relationship with traditional suites of applications on their computers, this kind of system could offer gamers a simple two-way streaming service in the place of a traditional, expensive console: an inexpensive box able to stream sounds and images in one direction, and relay their instructions in the other, with a central piece of hardware doing all the intensive work, just like the machinery that powers an internet search engine or any other remote service.

It's a notion that is remarkably close to becoming a reality. At the 2009 Game Developers Conference, for instance, a service called OnLive was announced, complete with a new kind of domestic gaming box that its makers dubbed the MicroConsole. Essentially a decoder of highly compressed signals sent via a broadband connection, the MicroConsole connects directly to a television and allows users to play any game they like by running it on a distant central data centre. The service will operate, initially, from five locations in America, but could theoretically be expanded much like any internet service company.

A fair amount of cynicism has surrounded the OnLive announcement, largely relating to the fact that efforts at 'centralised computing' have historically tended to end up either costing too much or suffering from too many reliability problems to be viable. But it's certain that sooner or later either OnLive itself or a service very like it will enter the marketplace and begin to compete. With regard to netbooks – relatively inexpensive and low-specification laptop computers designed mainly for online use – the fastest growing area of the modern computer market, the notion of delivering all kinds of remote gaming services to consumers is unlikely to go away.

At this point, it's worth sounding several notes of caution. New technology is marvellous to wonder at, and in the realm of gaming it can often border on the miraculous – this kind of delight being one of gaming's defining attributes. At the same time, however, change is never driven only by what is theoretically possible, or even by what is most exciting or transforming; there is also the weight of the past and of the fault lines, controversies and conflicts within any industry or medium.

Although the games industry is now starting to become a truly global phenomenon, it has traditionally been divided along a number of rigid and surprisingly impermeable regional lines. Throughout its history, gaming has been divided between, broadly, West and East, with America and Europe following a very different model to Asia – and Japan and Korea following their own idiosyncratic, and extremely influential, patterns within this.

The reasons for such extremes of regional variation relate to wealth, technological infrastructure, tradition and politics. China and Korea have traditionally enjoyed cheap, plentiful internet access, but have had low personal ownership rates of computers and little individual purchasing power, making online games the great money-spinners (Korea also had for many years a number of incredibly punitive taxes on all Japanese imports). Japan, the birthplace of the console, has always been intensely patriotic in its gaming – and curiously obsessed with internet applications

221

for mobile phones for which the internal market is huge, but for which there is almost no international demand. America and Europe, meanwhile, have emphasised domestic play on both computers and consoles, with high purchase rates of expensive blockbusting games and a reputation for innovation and craftsmanship matched only by the elite Japanese firms.

This compartmentalisation is finally starting to break down. Hardware has, since the early triumph of Japanese consoles, always spanned international boundaries; but now software hits are also drawing large numbers of players from across both the Western and Eastern markets. Moreover, gamers are finding themselves less limited by local technology, and by personal income, as the battle shifts from technical innovation to accessories, downloads and the construction of social forms of gaming and brands that can be carried across multiple formats.

This is not to say that worldwide gaming will entirely converge any time soon: in emerging markets, such as China, most people still don't own their own computers. But it is increasingly likely that global competition will bring into play an almost Darwinian principle, with local companies likely to fall under the weight of increased foreign competition. This may prove the case, for instance, in the Korean online gaming market, which has traditionally evolved in isolation from both the West and Japan and placed a strong emphasis on the 'grind' of levelling up with friends rather than more sophisticated tactical considerations. As markets merge online, the South-East Asian sector is likely to consolidate, with Korea losing out to China's rapidly growing player community and its entrepreneurial levels of innovation.

Similarly, Europe at the moment lacks any truly dominant regional online games specialist.

Like so much of digital culture, these transitions are bound up with a number of urgent and specific questions that governments and regulators need to address. In an age where virtual worlds span nations and even continents, and players collectively earn and exchange billions of dollars through them, what is the status of virtual property and money? What is the status of goods and services that individuals have bought, or created themselves, within this environment? And how can any of this be enforced, or a method of taxing income relating to virtual items be introduced?

Couple this to continuing concerns over violence, sexual content, censorship and addiction, and you have one melancholy certainty for the future of gaming: future controversies and scandals are likely to emerge on a scale beyond anything we've seen so far. Video games have been blamed before for teen violence, for falling educational standards and for disengaging players from the societies they live in – and with games growing ever more powerful and ubiquitous, there's every chance that this youngest of modern media will become the scapegoat for the most headline-grabbing of future controversies.

Such objections are not entirely irrational. Change is always traumatic, and games are a profound engine of change, both generationally and across society as a whole. Games are exceptionally powerful, and this power will be abused and exploited, not least by manufacturers seeking easy publicity by plumbing the depths of an ever-broadening audience's tastes. Some games have already been banned for, among other things, simulating the stalking and rape of women, for excessive violence and for scenes of distressing cruelty – none of which are peculiar to video games, or common in games, but which take on an understandable extra dimension of distaste because a player is actually 'doing' rather than merely watching. Censorship debates and panics will continue, as will the still more intractable debate over addiction – for which the only real solutions are vigilance, education and the identification of other underlying issues.

By their very nature, video games represent a profound challenge to many existing social assumptions and structures, not least of which is the very notion of society as something defined by proximity and geography rather than the transnational web of affiliations of many in-game communities. Along with the increasing ubiquity of the internet, some people will undoubtedly become conflicted between the demands of their virtual and their real lives – and one of the major challenges of the present century will be working out how to deal with this migration of attention, interest, effort and expenditure away from the actual and local towards the incorporeal and the diffuse. It's a challenge that games, if correctly understood, can help with rather than hinder, for it's within games that many of the most striking innovations in online community management are occurring: developments geared to making virtual relationships fairer, more transparent and more rewarding. Actuality will have to work hard to keep up with virtuality, but this may well be no bad thing.

One striking point, here, is that every major game world in existence is currently operated by a private corporation, which, given the sheer number of people playing some games and the value they attach to their virtual existence, puts a great deal of power into the hands of organisations whose primary motivation is simply profit. Such profits are of course bound up with keeping players happy, a powerful reason for maintaining a high quality and integrity of service. But keeping people happy does not represent anything like the full potential of virtual worlds, and if we are to understand and exploit their potential fully, there is great scope for research organisations, universities and even governments to step into this arena and begin large-scale gaming ventures. Games have already proved they can offer by far the most effective and appealing techniques for organising meaningful virtual communities, and if the notion that they somehow cannot be serious can be got out of the way, the potential of not-for-profit gaming is immense.

A virtual voting system could, for instance, be hugely effective at increasing voter participation and awareness, as could information projects connected to everything from energy visualisation to community collaboration and consultation on laws and local spending. Already, individual avatars can number among the most valuable – and certainly the most intimate and valued – of some people's possessions; and we are not too far away from a time when people may see their unique online embodiment as a literal extension of their self, complete with possessions, attributes and a legally protected right to exist and undertake economic activity. In this context, the question of who controls and regulates such a realm – a government, a private company, or even a distinct international authority – is a question with powerful consequences for an age thick with virtual work as well as play.

The economist Edward Castronova is one vocal advocate of government and university investment in virtual game worlds, in part because of his own Catholic faith and his belief that a 'good life' – either virtual or real – must be larger and distinct from a merely enjoyable, comfortable one. Virtual worlds can be hugely seductive, and there is a fine line between having life-enhancing experiences within them and seeking out virtual experiences in order to escape the challenges of living a real life. With the possibilities for distraction and escape more potent than they have ever been, it has correspondingly never been more important to educate people about balancing their lives between all the opportunities for distraction and participation on offer – and ensuring that the vulnerable are protected, and the pathological identified and helped.

What, finally, of other media in a digital age? In mid-2009, I was part of a panel of five interviewers who spent two hours discussing with Mark Thompson, Director-General of the BBC, his perspective on the future evolution of the media as a whole. Did he worry about younger people tuning in and dropping out of the established media world, and losing out in consequence? 'If one looks at media throughout the ages,' he replied, 'people always fear total substitution: the horse buggy to automobile. Actually, that doesn't seem to be the way things play out. Books, it turns out, have a wonderful future in the digital age. People thought television would kill off radio. Why on earth would you want a radio when television can give you everything a radio gives you plus pictures, they asked – quite wrongly as it turned out. Then television was going to kill cinema. But what we've actually seen is their co-existence, and the reorganising of interrelationships between media as you go. I believe that physical newspapers are likely to be with us twenty to thirty years from now – although the economics of newspapers will probably change beyond recognition, and there will almost certainly be fewer. Similarly, the passive experience of television is getting better and better.'

Thompson's answer echoes a theory first stated by the German thinker Wolfgang Riepl in 1913. Riepl, a newspaper editor, observed that when it came to media, technological advances never entailed the wholesale replacement of an existing form with an entirely new one, as it had done, for instance, in fields such as transport (where the horse was entirely replaced by the railway and, later, the automobile) or warfare (where gunpowder rendered bows and arrows redundant). Instead, what he called convergence occurred, with each medium impacting upon but not replacing the other, and a new system of usage involving both media gradually emerging. Today, those who fear that the ascendancy of video games – or any other medium – will impoverish the world by driving out older forms of expression should take comfort from Riepl's so-called 'law', which has proved remarkably prescient over the course of almost a hundred years.

Like society itself, media are better understood as a constantly evolving and interlocking system than as a discrete series of trends and ventures. There is competition within such a system, of course, sometimes of a brutally Darwinian nature. But there are also synergies and shared fundamentals, the most significant of which is the users themselves, whose natures have not shifted perceptibly over the millennia between the invention of writing and the present day, let alone between the creation of cinema and the birth of the games console. Older media must continue to adapt, and governments, societies and families must continue to support and value them. But the apparent war between different media is emphatically not a struggle for the human soul between debasing and ennobling tendencies. There is bad and good in each medium, as well as great power, and the recipe for progress remains much the same as it has always been: investigation, rigour, understanding, specificity, context, education and, perhaps above all, the refusal to succumb to glib hysteria.

Just as the printed word, recorded music and moving images have already done, the interactive art that is video gaming will continue to develop alongside its audience, serving both the best and the worst of them. It is rapidly becoming one of the central ways in which we seek to understand (and distract, and delight) ourselves in the twenty-first century, and one of the most important resources we have for understanding and creating the kinds of business and communications strategies that are likely to dominate the next few decades. Above all, for the coming generations – for whom the world before video games will seem as remote a past as one without cinema does to us – the best gift we can bequeath is a muscular and discerning critical engagement.

Epilogue

In June 1938, the world was less than eighteen months away from what would prove to be the bloodiest conflict in human history, the Second World War. In Europe, Hitler's Germany had recently annexed Austria and was poised to add Czechoslovakia to its swelling empire, while dictators held sway over Spain and Italy. In the east, Japan was perpetrating a brutal war of invasion against mainland China, while Stalin's Soviet Union had since 1937 shot or transported more than a million people in the Great Purge. Meanwhile, in the city of Leiden in the southern Netherlands, a historian was completing his work on a book that contained these words:

> For many years the conviction has grown upon me that civilization arises and unfolds in and as play . . . Civilization will, in a sense, always be played according to certain rules, and true civilization will always demand fair play. Fair play is nothing less than good faith expressed in play terms. Hence the cheat or the spoil-sport shatters civilization itself. To be a sound culture-creating force this play-element must

be pure. It must not consist in the darkening or debasing of standards set up by reason, faith or humanity. It must not be a false seeming, a masking of political purposes behind the illusion of genuine play-forms. True play knows no propaganda; its aim is in itself, and its familiar spirit is happy inspiration.

The writer was Johan Huizinga, one of the greatest and most influential of cultural historians. In 1942 he was taken hostage by the Nazis and imprisoned, dying in 1945 from ill health. Yet he chose, in his last published work, to address a topic that all his life had seemed to him of the most profound human significance – that of play.

Huizinga entitled his book *Homo Ludens: A Study of the Play-Element in Culture* (*Homo Ludens* means 'Man the Player'). Its central thesis was that in the human sense of fun there was something that lay outside of, and provided a vital counterbalance to, the potentially dark forces of ambition, discipline and reason. Writing on the eve of one of the bleakest decades in human history, Huizinga argued that true civilisation demanded the presence of 'happy inspiration' within even the most serious matters of justice, government, warfare and education. Far from seeing play as irrelevant at such a time, it seemed to him all the more urgent to make the case for the vital force of this 'play-element' in a world that had proved all too easily manipulated by the postures of authoritarian ideology.

Huizinga, whose work has become a touchstone for many writers on the theory of games, could scarcely have imagined what this world might hold six decades after his death. Yet at least some of his hopes have proved prophetic. Today, the swelling pressure of play can be felt across the world in business, in communications, in politics, in leisure: a discipline capable of smuggling the art back into science, and the human touch back into the mirthless and dogmatic.

Inequalities of wealth and opportunity have kept this movement mainly confined to more developed nations thus far, yet this pressure remains an essentially popular one. It's more than an economic fact that the allure of conventional consumer products, and of conventional earning opportunities, is increasingly being trumped among millions of people by a very different hierarchy of priorities. These games must somehow be paid for, of course, as well as produced, but the impulses they satisfy and stir up are quite a different thing to the worthy world of 'work' as it was conceived at the beginning of the modern era. Video games symbolise the ongoing story of the development of the mass media, writ larger than ever before: the human hunger for tales, for fiction, for the playful and the titillating, for delight and distraction.

For all their economic potential, there is something essentially subversive in games that has the force to crack open even the great playground of capitalism. Games tend to expose the element of play in all things: the fantasy of money, the magical abstractions of a name. They represent a refuge from the world, too, with the potential to be more than merely an exercise in evasion and irresponsibility: something that can function both as a critique of what is lacking in many lives and as a channel through which those lives might be changed.

If video games are at root both a popular and a populist art, with all the opportunities for pandering and crudity that that implies, they are also uniquely refined in their dedication not simply to visceral gratification, but to abstract and defiantly individual delight. What we learn about ourselves through them may change the way we conceive of, and seek to govern, the societies we inhabit; and it will certainly transform the ways in which we understand and regulate everything from property to employment to identity.

Johan Huizinga was above all a historian of the Middle Ages, a period that he described as 'brimful of play: the joyous and unbuttoned play of the people, full of pagan elements that had lost their sacred significance and been transformed into jesting and buffoonery, or the solemn and pompous play of chivalry'. What might he have thought, had he had a glimpse of the world a century after his death and been able to watch countless people spending their time within quasi-medieval fictional worlds, whiling away their afternoons gathering virtual resources to be used in the crafting of armour or weapons, or in funding a fine castle for their virtual selves to inhabit? He would, perhaps, have glimpsed in this strange and gleefully anachronistic pillaging of times past a cultural force not so different to old Europe's own 'joyous and unbuttoned' borrowings in the service of fun. And he couldn't fail to notice just how profound an influence certain medieval, or pseudo-medieval, notions have had on these worlds, from guilds and trades to chivalry and legends.

Huizinga might have been appalled, delighted or merely bemused by the curious reversals inherent in any virtual world – people undertaking menial and entirely fictional tasks in order to gain the kind of simple satisfactions absent from the daily texture of their lives. Then again, it has always been the essential character of play that its objectives are valued as they are experienced, and not for anything inherent or enduring in them, a fact close to the heart of its ability to supplant worldly logic with an altogether more mercurial set of relations.

In the end, we share one question in common with every other age: will our creations seduce us away from the task of making the world we are born into a better one; or can they help us to civilise it and ourselves? Games alone cannot teach us what it means to live a good life any more than they can by themselves drive us into narcissism or failure. But they can, if we are able to understand and use them well enough, play a powerful part in our struggle to live both more happily and better.

Bibliography
and ludography

Books

Amis, Martin, *Invasion of the Space Invaders* (London: Hutchinson, 1982)

Berens, Kate and Howard, Geoff, *The Rough Guide to Videogames* (London: Rough Guides, 2008)

Crawford, Chris, *The Art of Computer Game Design* (Berkeley, CA: Osborne, 1984) – an electronic version of the text is available online at www.vancouver.wsu.edu/fac/peabody/game-book/Coverpage.html

Csikszentmihalyi, Mihaly, *Flow: The Psychology of Optimal Experience* (London: Harper Perennial, 1991)

Dibbell, Julian, *Play Money, Or, How I Quit My Day Job and Made Millions Trading Virtual Loot* (New York: Basic Books, 2006) – a blog and other materials relating to the book can be found online at www.juliandibbell.com/playmoney/

Duhamel, Georges, *America the Menace: Scenes from the Life of the Future*, translated by Charles Miner Thompson (London: Allen & Unwin, 1931)

Greenfield, Susan, *iD: The Quest for Identity in the 21st Century* (London: Sceptre, 2008)

Huizinga, Johan, *Homo Ludens: A Study of the Play-Element in Culture* (London: Routledge & Kegan Paul, 1949)

Koster, Raph, *A Theory of Fun for Game Design* (Phoenix, Arizona: Paraglyph Press, 2005)

McAllister, Graham and White, Gareth, 'Video Game Development and User Experience' in Regina Bernhaupt (ed.), *Evaluating User Experience in Games* (London: Springer Verlag, 2009)

Rossignol, Jim, *This Gaming Life: Travels in Three Cities* (Ann Arbor, MI: University of Michigan Press, 2008)

Plato, *Phaedrus*, full text online at http://classics.mit.edu/Plato/phaedrus.html

Poole, Steven, *Trigger Happy* (London: Fourth Estate, 2000) – an electronic version of the text is available online at steven-poole.net/trigger happy/

Singer, Peter W., *Wired for War: The Robotics Revolution and Conflict in the 21st Century* (New York: Penguin Press, 2009)

Szymanski, Stefan, *Playbooks and Checkbooks: An Introduction to the Economics of Modern Sports* (Princeton, NJ: Princeton University Press, 2009)

Wright, Evan, *Generation Kill: Living Dangerously on the Road to Baghdad with the Ultraviolent Marines of Bravo Company* (London and New York: Bantam, 2004)

Articles, reports and presentations

Alderman, Naomi, 'Computer Games are Good for You', *Guardian*, 11 November 2008; <http://www.guardian.co.uk/technology/2008/nov/11/computer-game-addiction-diablo-9-11>

Anderson, Craig A; Sakamoto, Akira; Gentile, Douglas A; Ihori, Nobuko; Shibuya, Akiko; Yukawa, Shintaro; Naito, Mayumi; Kobayashi, Kumiko, 'Longitudinal Effects of Violent Video Games on Aggression in Japan and the United States', *Pediatrics*, November 2008, Volume 122; <http://pediatrics.aappublications.org/cgi/ content/abstract/122/5/e1067>

Balicer, Ran D, 'Modeling infectious diseases dissemination through online role-playing games', *Epidemiology*, March 2007, Volume18, Issue 2; <http://journals.lww.com/epidem/Abstract/2007/03000/Modeling_Infectious_Diseases_Disseminaton_Throgh.15.aspx>

Bartle, Richard, 'Virtual Worlds: Why People Play', 2005; <http://mud.co.uk/richard/papers.htm>

Brand, Stewart, 'Spacewar! Fanatic Life and Symbolic Death Among the Computer Bums', *Rolling Stone*, 7 December 1972; <http://www.wheels.org/spacewar/stone/rolling_stone.html>

Byron, Tanya, 'Safe Children in a Digital World: The Report of the Byron Review', June 2008; <http://www.dcsf.gov.uk/byron review/>

Castronova, Edward, 'Virtual Worlds: A First-Hand Account of Market and Society on the Cyberian Frontier', *The Gruter Institute Working Papers on Law, Economics, and Evolutionary Biology*, 2001, Volume 2, Article 1; <http://www.bepress.com/giwp/default/vol2/iss1/art1>

Castronova, Edward and Fairfield, Joshua, 'Dragon Kill Points: A Summary White Paper', January 2007; <http://ssrn.com/abstract=958945>

Chatfield, Tom, 'Rage Against the Machines', *Prospect* magazine, June 2008; <http://www.prospectmagazine.co.uk/2008/06/rageagainstthemachines/>

Chatfield, Tom, 'Screen Test', *New Statesman*, 30 April 2009; <http://www.newstatesman.com/ideas/2009/05/video-games-industry-art-film>

Chatfield, Tom, 'Videogames Now Outperform Hollywood Movies', *Observer*, 27 September 2009; <http://www.guardian.co.uk/technology/gamesblog/2009/sep/27/videogames-hollywood>

Ellis, Hilary; Heppell, Stephen; Kirriemuir, John; Krotoski, Aleks; McFarlane, Angela, 'Unlimited Learning: Computer and Video Games in the Learning Landscape', September 2006; <http://www.elspa.com/assets/files/u/unlimitedlearningtheroleof-computerandvideogamesint_344.pdf>

Ferguson, Christopher John, 'The Good, The Bad and the Ugly: A Meta-analytic Review of Positive and Negative Effects of Violent Video Games', *Psychiatric Quarterly*, December 2007, Volume 78, Number 4; <http://www.springerlink.com/content/66217176984x7477/fulltext.pdf>

Ferguson, Christopher John, 'The School Shooting/Violent Video Game Link: Causal Link or Moral Panic?', *Journal of Investigative Psychology and Offender Profiling*, December 2008, Volume 5, Issue 1-2: <http://www3.interscience.wiley.com/cgi-bin/fulltext/121556773 /PDFSTART>

Gentile, Douglas A, 'Pathological Video Game Use among Youth 8 to 18: A National Study', *Psychological Science*, 22 September 2008; <http://www.drdouglas.org/drdpdfs/Gentile_Pathological_VG_Use_in_press.pdf>

Goldsmith, Jeffrey, 'This Is Your Brain on Tetris', *Wired*, May 1994; <http://www.wired.com/wired/archive/2.05/tetris.html>

Jo Kim, Amy, 'Putting the Fun in Functional: Applying Game Mechanics to Functional Software', Google Tech Talks, January 2009; <http://www.youtube.com/watch?v=ihUt-163gZI>

Johnson, Boris, 'The Writing is on the Wall – Computer Games Rot the Brain', *Daily Telegraph*, 28 December 2006; <http://www.telegraph.co.uk/comment/personal-view/3635699/The-writing-is-on-the-wall—-computer-games-rot-the-brain.html>

Lanchester, John, 'Is it Art?', *London Review of Books*, 1 January 2009; <http://www.lrb.co.uk/v31/n01/lanc01_.html>

Lazzaro, Nicole, 'Why We Play Games: Four Keys to More Emotion Without Story', 8 March, 2004; available via www.xeodesign.com

Lehdonvirta, Vili, 'Virtual Item Sales as a Revenue Model: Identifying Attributes that Drive Purchase Decisions', *Electronic Commerce Research*, June 2009, Volume 9, Numbers 1–2; <http://www.springerlink.com/content/055100248749q2v5/fulltext.pdf>

Lehtonen, Liz, 'Complexity in Games: What Game Developers Need to Know', unpublished thesis, 2007; available upon request via http://liz.lehtonen.googlepages.com/portfolio

Lewitt, Adam, 'Mass Killer "Rejected" by Girl at Party', *Sunday Times*, 15 March 2009; <http://www.timesonline.co.uk/tol/news/world/europe/article5908602.ece>

Lofgren, Eric T and Fefferman, Nina H, 'The Untapped Potential of Virtual Game Worlds to Shed Light on Real World Epidemics', *Lancet, Infectious Diseases*, September 2007, Volume 7, Issue 9; <http://terranova.blogs.com/s14733099077021283.pdf>

Martin, Adam and Chatfield, Tom (eds), 'Alternate Reality Games White Paper', 2006, written for the International Game Developers Association ARG Special Interest Group; <http://www.igda.org/ arg/resources/IGDA-AlternateReality Games-Whitepaper-2006.pdf>

Martin, Tim, 'Endpaper – Fiction Reaches a New Level', *Daily*

Telegraph, 7 May 2009; <http://www.telegraph.co.uk/culture
/books/ bookreviews/5291671/Endpaper---Fiction-reaches-a-new-
level.html>

PricewaterhouseCoopers, 'Global Entertainment and Media
Outlook: 2009–2013', report of 2009; available via
www.pwc.com/gx/en/ global-entertainment-media-outlook

Reeves, Byron; Malone, Thomas W and O'Driscoll, Tony,
'Leadership's Online Labs', *Harvard Business Review*, May 2008;
<http://hbr.harvardbusiness.org/2008/05/leaderships-online-
labs/ar/1>

Reeves, Byron, 'Welcome to an Exploration of: Multiplayer Games,
Virtual Worlds and Energy Efficiency', November 2008; video
viewable on YouTube at www.youtube.com/watch?v=dDR0-
QgqiEk

Scruton, Roger, 'Can Virtual Life Take over from Real Life?', *Sunday
Times*, 16 November 2008; <http://technology.timesonline.co.uk
/tol/news/tech_and_web/the_web/article5139532.ece>

Thier, David, 'World of Warcraft Shines Light on Terror Tactics',
Wired, 20 March 2008; <http://www.wired.com/gaming/virtual-
worlds/ news/2008/03/wow_terror>

Tieman, Ross, 'Recruits Fired up by Virtual Rivalry', *Financial Times*,
3 May 2009; online via archive search at www.ft.com

Watts, Peter, 'Tunnel 228: Theatre for the Playstation
Generation',*The Big Smoke* blog for *Time Out London*, 20 May
2009; <http://www.timeout.com/london/big smoke/blog/7779/
Tunnel_228-theatre_for_the_Playstation_generation.html>

Magazines, websites and other resources

The Daedalus Project, the website at www.nickyee.com/daedalus
contains numerous important articles and data relating to Nick
Yee's long-running survey of MMO players

Edge magazine (Future Publishing, UK), games news, reviews and
forums; <http://www.edge-online.com>

Entertainment and Leisure Software Publishers Association, British
membership association for the computer and video games
industry, with many reports and data resources;
<http://www.elspa.com>

Entertainment software association, US association serving games publishers; <http://www.theesa.com/about/index.asp>

Gamasutra, an indispensable website for games developers; <http://www.gamasutra.com>

GamerDNA, a social media company for gamers; <http://www.gamerdna.com>

Games investor consulting; their website at www.gamesinvestor.com contains invaluable reports on games industry business models, and reports on the history and current state of the industry

Games for Change (G4C), a US-based community and movement dedicated to using games for the purposes of social change; <http://www.gamesforchange.org>

Hot Milky Drink, Derek Robertson's blog on the potentials of games as learning tools; <http://hotmilkydrink.typepad.com/>

Jason Rohrer, his homepage hosts games, writing and more; <http://hcsoftware.sourceforge.net/jason-rohrer/>

Kongregate, one of the best of the growing number of Flash gaming sites; <http://www.kongregate.com>

Negative Gamer, a refreshingly opinionated blog on what the gaming world ought to be doing better; <http://negativegamer.com>

Pew Internet & American Life Project, free data and analysis on trends shaping America and the world, with detailed reports on new media usage; <http://www.pewinternet.org>

Seriosity, a consulting company applying game strategies to other businesses; <http://www.seriosity.com>

Slate magazine (The Washington Post Company), news, politics and culture, including incisive tech commentary: <http://www.slate.com>

Stephanie Rothenberg, this artist's website explores the boundaries between work and play, and virtual and real lives; <http://www.pan-o-matic.com>

T-machine blog, games development blog specialising in MMOs and iPhone development; <http://t-machine.org/>

Terra Nova, influential collaborative blog on virtual worlds and virtual economics; <http://terranova.blogs.com/>

Wired magazine (Condé Nast) explores the effects of technology on life; <http://www.wired.com>

Games and virtual worlds

America's Army, US Army & Ubisoft, 2002 (Windows PC, Mac OS, Linux)

BioShock, 2K Games, 2007 (Windows PX, Xbox 360, PlayStation 3, Mac OS)

Boom Blox, Electronic Arts, 2008 (Wii, Mobile, N-Gage 2.0)

Cloud, USC Interactive Media Division, 2005 (Windows PC)

Dr Kawashima's Brain Training, Nintendo, 2005 (Nintendo DS)

Doom, id Software, 1993 (MS-DOS PC)

Darfur is Dying, mtvU, 2006 (Web browser)

EVE Online, CCP Games, 2003 (Windows PC, Mac OS)

EverQuest, Sony Online Entertainment, 1999 (Windows PC, Mac OS)

fl0w, Sony Computer Entertainment, 2006 (PlayStation 3, PSP)

Flower, Sony Computer Entertainment, 2009 (PlayStation 3)

Gator Six, Will Interactive/US Army, 2005 (specialist interactive training)

Ghostbusters; The Video Game, Atari, 2009 (Windows PC, Nintendo DS, PSP, Play Station 2, PlayStation 3, Wii, Xbox 360)

Grand Theft Auto IV, Rockstar Games, 2008 (PlayStation 3, Xbox 360, Windows PC)

Guitar Hero, RedOctane/MTV Games, 2005 (PlayStation 2)

How Big is Your Brain?, Playfish, 2008 (Web Browser, iPhone)

I Dig It, InMotion Software, 2009 (iPhone)

Legend of Mir 3, WeMade Entertainment, 2009 (Windows PC)

Medal of Honor, Electronic Arts, 1999 (PlayStation)

M.U.L.E., Elecronic Arts/Ariolasoft, 1983 (Atari 400/800)

Minesweeper, Microsoft, 1990 (Windows PC)

Moshi Monsters, Mind Candy, 2008 (Web Browser)

MUD (Multi-User Dungeon), Essex University network, 1980 (DEC PDP-10)

Nintendogs, Nintendo, 2005 (Nintendo DS)

Overlord, Codemasters, 2007 (Xbox 360, Windows PC, PlayStation 3)

Pac-Man, Namco, 1980 (Arcade cabinet)

Passage, Jason Rohrer, 2007 (Windows PC, Mac OS, GNU/Linux)

Pokémon, Nintendo, 1996 (Game Boy)

Pong, Atari, 1972 (Arcade cabinet)

Psychonauts, Majesco Entertainment, 2005 (Xbox, Windows PC, PlayStation 2)

Restaurant City, Playfish, 2009 (Web browser)

Rock Band, MTV Games/Electronic Arts, 2007 (PlayStation 2, PlayStation 3, Xbox 360, Wii)

Second Life, Linden Lab, 2003 (Windows PC, Mac OS, Linux)

SingStar, Sony Computer Entertainment Europe, 2004 (PlayStation 2)

Space Invaders, Midway, 1978 (Arcade cabinet)

Spacewar!, MIT, 1962 (DEC PDP-1)

Star Wars Galaxies, LucasArts, 2003 (Windows PC)

Starcraft, Blizzard Entertainment, 1998 (Windows PC, Mac OS)

Super Mario Brothers, Nintendo, 1985 (Nintendo Entertainment System)

Tetris, Nintendo, 1989 (Game Boy)

The Hitchhiker's Guide to the Galaxy, Infocom, 1984 (Apple II, Macintosh, Commodore 64, Amiga, Atari 8-bit and ST, IBM PC)

The Legend of Sword and Fairy, Softstar Entertainment, 1995 (Windows & DOS PC)

The Sims, Electronic Arts, 2000 (Windows PC, Mac OS, Linux, PlayStation 2, Xbox, GameCube)

Ultima Online, Electronic Arts, 1997 (Windows PC)

Wii Play, Nintendo, 2006 (Wii)

World of Warcraft, Blizzard Entertainment, 2004 (Windows PC, Mac OS)

Zelda Two: The Adventure of Link, Nintendo, 1987 (Nintendo Entertainment System)

Acknowledgements

A lot of people have given freely of their time, expertise and good will during the writing of this book, and it couldn't exist without them. Thank you all. All errors, of course, are the author's own, while most of the best ideas were first gleaned in conversation with one or more of the people listed below.

Thanks first of all to my darling wife, Cat, without whose patience, support and near-infinite capacity for reading first and second drafts this book would never have made it to fruition in the first place. Thanks, too, to her alter ego Sangla for companionship and expert healing in the more hazardous parts of Azeroth.

This book wouldn't have existed without the insight, expertise and considerable efforts of Robert Dudley, who first suggested I write it and went on to make this idea a reality. I would also like to thank Jon Elek for his ongoing enthusiasm, advice and representations on my behalf.

I'm hugely grateful, too, to David Goodhart, David Hanger and everyone else at *Prospect* magazine, who both published my articles in the first place and supported me throughout my writing with consideration, generosity and (most crucially of all) time away from my desk. The whole *Prospect* editorial team have been instrumental in helping me to think and to write better, and in sending a steady stream of gaming ideas and queries my way: thank you, Tom, James, Hilly, Susha, Mary, Jonathan, Brian, David.

Editorially, working with the Virgin team – Louisa and Sophia – and my copy editor Jane has been a delight, especially for someone who spends so much time sitting behind an editorial desk themselves. Thanks both to them, and to everyone else who has put so much effort into making this book look beautiful and persuading people to read it: Jessica, Vickie, Lucy, and everyone and anyone else at Random House who I've failed to notice working on my behalf.

I've interviewed and talked to a huge number of people for this book, not all of whom have even made it into this final cut (my fault, not theirs). One of the greatest pleasures of writing about the games industry has been the sheer goodwill and passion I've encountered amongst those working in and around it, and their willingness to explain themselves for hours to – or to swap emails and Skype calls with – a persistent stranger with a Dictaphone and a coffee habit. A thousand thanks and more to those inside, around and interested in all matters fun-related, including:

Naomi Alderman, Richard Bartle, Adam 'Mogwai' Brouwer, Michael Bywater, Peter Bazalgette, Edward Castronova, Jenova Chen, Timothy Crosby, Julian Dibbell, Jim Greer, Dawn Hallybone, Adrian Hon, Rupert Humphries, Raph Koster, Liz

& Ville Lehtonen, Sam Leith, Simon Levene, Jason 'Jagarr' & Kim 'Lambytoes' Long, Nicholas Lovell, Adam Martin, Jon 'Magicmoocow' Matheson (aka Baxie), Graham McAllister, Craig McKechnie & the Hooligans, Philip Oliver, Tim Phillips, Rhianna Pratchett, Michael Rawlinson, Derek Robertson, Kristian Segerstråle, Suzanne Seggerman, Michael Smith, Linda Snow, Justin Villiers, Peter Watts, David Wortley, Nick Yee, Riccardo Zacconi ...

Plus numberless, nameless others who have found themselves cornered by me at parties and in cafés and compelled to talk about games. It's been a pleasure and a privilege.

Index

3D modelling 115, 116
9/11 attacks (2001) 80
2001: a Space Odyssey (film) 113
Acel Group 216
achievement 4
Acorn Computers 1
addiction 71–8, 223
'adventure' games 1, 2
advertising 30, 32, 33, 114, 210, 217, 219
Alderman, Naomi 80
alienation 78
Amazon 90, 219
America 69, 222
America's Army 190–91, 194
Amstrad 95
Anatomy of Care 196–7
Apple 213
    App Store 213, 214
Arcade (film) 87
arcade games 19, 21
Aristotle 125
Assyrians 1
Atari 18, 19, 21, 22

400 home computer 11
Australia 69
Austria 229
Avatar (film) 44
avatars 43–4, 90, 141, 143, 168–9, 225
Aykroyd, Dan 137

Baer, Ralph 19
Bakker, Keith 77–8
Balicer, Ran D 174–5
Ballard, J G 45
Bartle, Richard 45–9, 51, 101
'Bartle quotient' 48
'Bartle Test of Gamer Psychology' 48
BBC Micro Model B 1
Beatles, the 135, 136
Beatles: Rock Band, The 135
Bebo 89, 212
Berry, Dani Bunten 10
Bhagavad Gita 44
Bhagavata Purana 44
Bioshock 119

BitTorrent 216
Blair, Charles 176
Blitz Games Studios 114–15
  TruSim division 198
Blu-ray 27, 137, 218
board games 4, 6, 10, 13, 62,
  91
Boom Blox 138
brain-training games 202, 205,
  206
Brouwer, Adam 95–102
BSkyB 218
bullying
  cyber-bullies 63
  school 77
Bushnell, Nolan 18
Byron, Dr Tanya: *Safer Children
  in a Digital World* report 84

calculators 28
Cameron, James 44–5
Campbell, Joseph 46
Canada 69
Cartoon Network 49
Castronova, Edward 166–74,
  177, 226
  'Virtual Worlds: A First-Hand
  Account of Market and
  Society on the Cyberian
  Frontier' 167
casual gaming 33–7, 210–12
CDs 218
censorship 70, 224
Chen, Jenova 120–25
Cheshire, Bob 115
child abusers 63

children
  and censorship of violent
    media 70
  as video game players 58, 62,
    63–5, 75, 79
China 221, 222, 229
Chronotron 129
cinema 20, 57, 111–12, 227,
  228
  Kubrick's inventions 113–14
civilisation 229, 230
Clarke, Arthur C 13, 14–15
clay modelling 115
Climax 119
Cloud 121
'cloud computing' 219–20
Codemaster 119
collaboration 2, 3, 6, 7, 177
collecting 164
communication(s) 55, 78, 97,
  108, 109, 189, 209
competition 6, 7, 11, 139, 163,
  199, 206, 207, 228
  increased foreign 222
computers
  ability to run games/programs
    23–4
  browser-based fun 219
  computing activity conventions
    155–6
  constantly evolving 31
  double clicking 156
  drop-down menus 155
  freedom to browse the internet
    24
  gaming profits 24

interaction with 155–60
programming 15
slow, steady rise of 23
software 156
static as work environments
154–5
comScore 216, 217
concept art 115, 116, 123
Consolarium 201, 203
conversation 85, 103
cooperation 11, 60, 108, 139,
163, 179
copyright protection 28
'corrupted blood plague' 174,
176
Council of Stellar Management
(in *EVE Online*) 106–7
Crouse, Jeff 143
Csikszentmihalyi, Mihaly 42
customisation 164, 165
cyber-bullies 63
Czechoslovakia 229

Dabney, Ted 18
Dante's Inferno 87
Darfur is Dying 182–7
data mining 138
databases 155
depression 78
Diablo II 80
Diagnostic and Statistical
Manual of Mental Disorders
(DSM) 71, 73, 74
Dibbell, Julian: *Play Money*
148–9
digital age 28, 209, 226, 227

digital distribution 32
digital literacy 155
'digital natives' 210
digital revolution x, 38
Discworld 118
Disney, Walt: basic principles of
animation 115
Doom 188–9
dopamine 72
downloads 222
Dr Kawashima's Brain Training
202, 206
Dragon Kill Points (DKP) 177–9
'drone' aircraft (Reapers) 193–4
dry neural sensor technology
158
Duhamel, Georges: *Scenes from
the Life of the Future* 55–7
DVD drive 157
DVDs 27, 218

e-book readers 219
East Lothian council 204
eBay 60
economics 166, 170, 174
education 199–208, 223
    see also learning; training
educational aids 153
Electronic Arts 31, 49
email clients 155
email surveys 35
embodiment 44, 46, 141–2
emergency medicine games
197–9
emergent behaviours 11, 130
'end game' 94

energy costs 161–3
engagement 181, 186
Entertainment and Leisure
    Software Publishers
    Association 64
Entertainment Software
    Association of America 61
Entertainment Software Rating
    Board 62–3
environmental storytelling 119
Epidemiology journal 174
ergodic texts 200
Europe 222, 223
European Parliament 109
European Union (EU) 69
EVE Online 106–7, 129–31
EverQuest 103, 104–5, 167–8,
    177, 178
exchanges, gaming 164–5

Facebook ix, 33–4, 37, 89, 155,
    162, 212, 216
fair play 229
fantasy scenarios 140
Far Cry 2 68
feedback 35–7, 42, 72, 117, 164
    real-time sensory 211
Fefferman, Nina H 175
Ferguson, Dr Christopher John:
    'The Good, the Bad and the
    Ugly: A Meta-analytic
    Review of Positive and
    Negative Effects of Violent
    Video Games' 66
financial crisis (2008-date) 151,
    166

flow 42–3, 51, 122, 163–4,
    171
flOw 121, 122
Flower 121, 123–4, 126, 129
football 5, 7
'Four Keys to releasing emotions
    during play' 49–51
    altered states 50–51
    easy fun 50
    hard fun 50
    the people factor 51
full-body projections 14
fun
    browser-based 219
    Castronova on 170
    defined xiii, 8–9
    easy 50
    and engagement 181, 186
    hard 50
    modern games as 23
    Seggerman on 181

gambling 73, 74, 75, 77
Game Developers Conferences
    121, 220
gamerDNA 48
games
    history of 1, 3, 4
    rule-making 4–7, 11
    the universal urge to play 4
Games for Change 181, 187
'games for change' 186, 193
games charts 114
games consoles 210
    advancement in sudden leaps
    31

'console wars' 21
console-based television service 218–19
copyright protection 28
graphical and processing capacities 21
interface 157
and Japanese firms 21
Lovell on 215–16
the most valuable sector for gaming 33
Nintendo DS 202, 205–8
Nintendo Wii 23, 37, 91, 138, 156, 158, 160, 215, 217–18
Sony PlayStation 22
Sony PlayStation III 215, 218
Super Nintendo 200
'walled gardens' 24
Xbox 360 14, 215
Games for Health conference (Baltimore, 2008) 175
games-based learning 199–208
gaming industry
  digital distribution 32
  growth of 27–8, 30, 38, 113, 210–11
  invention of new methods and technology 114
  mid-priced movement 32, 33
  profitability 31–2
  publishers vs. developers 30–31
  regional variation 221–3
  risk 31, 32
  social and casual gaming 33–7
gaming mechanisms 164–5

Gator Six 195–6
Gentile, Dr Douglas A:
  'Pathological Video Game Use among Youth 8 to 18: A National Study' 73–5, 76, 79
Germany 67, 229
Ghostbusters 137
Ghostbusters films 137
Glow broadband network for schools 205
Goh, Oliver 161
gold farming 145, 146, 147, 149
Google 27, 162, 164, 211
governments 225
GPS-enabled gamers 211
Grand Theft Auto series 82–3
Grand Theft Auto IV (GTA IV) 29, 30, 81–2
'grandma gaming' 210
grandparents 62
graphics card 157
Great Purge 229
Greenfield, Susan 76
  iD: The Quest for identity in the 21st Century 72–3
griefing 176
group play 51
guilds 95–8, 100, 101, 104, 105, 175
Guinness World Records 191
Guitar Hero 91, 136, 156, 157, 203, 204

Hallybone, Dawn 206, 208
haptic devices 159

'hard-core' gaming 129
Harris polls 74
Harry Potter & The Deathly Hallows (Rowling) 29
Harvard Business Review 98–9
headsets 97, 158
hedonics 174
high-school shootings 67–9
Hitchhiker's Guide to the Galaxy, The xii
home game machine, world's first 19
hostage recovery scenarios 189
How Big is Your Brain? 34
Huizinga, Johan 233
  Homo Ludens: A Study of the Play-Element in Culture 229–32
human behaviour, and video games 165–79
human motivators 7
humour 9

I Dig It 213–14
I wish I were the moon 129
id Software 188
improvement 7
in-game interactions 7, 51
Inconvenient Truth, An (film) 186
Infocom 2
installation art 132
intellectual property 60
intelligent shared spaces 160–61
internationalism 5
internet 210, 224

browser 156
casual gaming 33–7, 210–12
computers' unrestricted freedom to browse 24
importance to younger children 64
online pursuits 83
and pornography 83
social relationships 89–90
the world's most important gaming arena 24
internet cafés 80–81
Invisible Threads 143
iPhones 212–14, 216
Iraq 191
invasion of (2003) 192, 195

Japan 221–2, 229
Japanese firms 21–3, 222
  professionalism 21
  rivalry between Nintendo and Sega 21–2
  success of Sony 22–3
Jo Kim, Amy 163–4
Johnson, Boris 56, 57
jumping 39–40

keyboard 157, 158, 159
Kindle 219
Kinect tracking box project 18
Korea 80–81, 221, 222
Koster, Raph 7–10, 39, 49
  A Theory of Fun for Game Design 7
Kretschmer, Tim 67, 68

Krishna (Indian deity) 44
Kubrick, Stanley 113–14
Kufeld, Albert W 17–18

laptops 210
Lazzaro, Nicole 49–50, 51
learning 6–9, 49, 94, 150, 153,
    157, 180, 181, 209
  contexts from learning 203
  experiential 10
  see also education; training
Learning and Teaching Scotland
    200, 201
Lee, Johnny Chung 160
Legend of Mir 3, The 60
Legend of Sword and Fairy, The
    120
Lehtonen, Liz and Ville 103–4
Levene, Simon 216–17
Lewitt, Adam 68
live art 131–4
Lord of the Rings series 113
Los Angeles Expo (2009) 13, 14
Lovell, Nicholas 215–16
Lucas, George 46
Lumière, Auguste and Louis
    111

McKechnie, Craig 99–100
Macropedia 216
Macs 23
Magnavox Odyssey 19, 20
Marine Doom 188–9
Mario games 39, 40
market locations 171
mass print media 20

Massachusetts Institute of
    Technology (MIT) 15–18
massively multiplayer online
    games (MMOs) 8, 48, 93,
    103, 105, 106, 138, 140,
    162, 176
Medal of Honor series 65
'meta-game' 105
microphones 51, 97
Microsoft 14, 216, 217
  enters console war 218
  programs 155
  Windows 42
military games 187–97
Mind Candy 63
Minesweeper 41–2
mobile phones 28, 34, 157–8,
    210, 212, 221–2
monitor 157
Moshi Monsters 63, 64
motion capture 14, 29, 137
motion sensitivity 23, 158, 159
motivation 149–51, 163, 177,
    179, 180, 184
mouse 156–9
MP3 players 28
MP3 recordings 136
MTV 37, 186
mtvU 186
MUD (Multi-User Dungeon)
    45
M.U.L.E. 10–11
multi-player games
  online 89, 169
  text-based 89
  time spent playing 29

Murdoch, Rupert 218
music
  interactive 135–6
  recorded 57, 228
MySpace 89, 155

National Adviser for Emerging
    Technologies and Learning,
    Scotland 200, 202
National Parenting Publications
    Award 64
natural sciences 169
Negative Gamer 75
netbooks 220–21
neurological control 211
NeuroSky 158, 159
newspapers 227
Nielsen Games 63
Nintendo 21, 22, 23, 27, 31, 39,
    76, 216
  brain-training games 205
  DS console 202, 205–8
  Super Nintendo 200
  Wii 37, 91, 138, 156, 158,
    160, 215, 217–18
Nintendogs 83
Norrath (a virtual world) 167,
    168
not-for-profit gaming 225
Novint Falcon controller 159
NP-hard problem ('non-
    deterministic polynomial
    hard' problem) 41–2

Oakdale Junior School, Essex
    205–8

Olympics 2
online community management
    224
online 'counter-culture' 110
online games
  creation of 3
  gaming community 29
  motivating, co-operative social
    tools 108
  players' achievements in
    29–30
  profitability 221
  reward distribution 177–9
OnLive service 220
OpenShaspa Home Energy Kit
    161–2
OpenShaspa system 161
Overlord series 119
Overlord: Dark Legend 119
Overlord: Minions 119
Overlord: Raising Hell 119
Overlord II 119

Pac–Man 20, 201
Pajitnov, Alexey 40, 41, 42
Palace, The 172
Pan European Game Information
    System (PEGI) 62–3
parents 63–4, 138
party games 91
Passage 126–8, 129
PCs 23
PDP-1 (Programmed Data
    Processor) 15, 16, 17
Pediatrics journal: 'Longitudinal
    Effects of Violent Video

Games on Aggression in Japan and the United States' 67

pentominos 41

performance art 130, 133

performance games 91

persistence 154

personalisation 154

Pet Society 36–7

pets
 'pet' games 83
 in *WoW* 94

Pew Internet/MacArthur Report on Teens, Video Games and Civics (2008) 90, 108–9

Pictionary 6–7

Pirate Bay website, The 109

Pirate Party 109

Pixar Studios 117

platform games 83

Plato: *Phaedrus* 55, 56

play, Huizinga on 229–30, 232

player motivations (Killer, Achiever, Explorer and Socialiser) 47–8, 49

Playfish 33–7

points 164

Pokémon series 83

political awareness 181

political issues 108–9

Pong 18–20

Poole, Steven 126
 Trigger Happy 125

pornography 83

Posner, Judge Richard A 70–71

Pratchett, Rhianna 117–19

Pratchett, Terry 117–18

prefrontal cortex 72

primal response patterns 163

Psychiatric Quarterly journal 66

psychological science 153

Psychological Science journal 73

Psychonauts 119–20

Punchdrunk theatre company 133–4

radio 20, 57–8, 227

'raiding missions' 97–8

RAM 157

Rama (Indian hero) 44

Ramayana 44

Ramis, Harold 137

ratings 63, 64, 65, 164

Rawlinson, Michael 64–5

reading 85

Real 216

real-time conversation 51

Reeves, Professor Byron 162–3

research organisations 225

Restaurant City 37

reward schedule 149–50

rewards 199, 206, 209

Riepl, Wolfgang 227

Riepl's law 227

Robertson, Derek 199–206

robots, military use of 194–5

Rock Band games 91, 135–6

Rohrer, Jason 126, 127–8

role-playing games 29, 45, 83

Rothenberg, Stephanie 143

Russell, Stephen 'Slug' 15–16, 22

scarcity 172, 173
Scottish education 199–205
Scruton, Roger 91–2, 101
Second Life 90, 118, 142–6
Second World War 229
Sega 21, 22, 23, 31
Segerstråle, Kristian 34–7
Seggerman, Suzanne 181–2, 186, 187, 193
self-expression 7, 43, 51, 94
Serious Games Institute, Coventry University 153, 161
Shining, The (film) 113–14
Sims, The series 83
SingStar 136
sketching 115
smartphones 219
Smith & Jones Centre, Amsterdam 77
Smith, Michael 63–4
Snow, Linda 207–8
social awareness 181
social networks 14, 24, 34, 83, 89, 154, 212, 217, 218
social problems 78
social sciences 153, 169, 180
Sony 22–3, 31, 95, 103, 104, 168, 216, 217, 218
    PlayStation 22
    PlayStation III 215, 218
sound 20, 112, 116, 157
South-East Asia sector 222
Soviet Union 229
Space Invaders 20, 201
Spacewar! (world's first true computer game) 16–18, 37

speakers 51
Spider-Man 3 (film) 29
Spielberg, Steven 14, 137–8
sports 5, 91
Star Trek series 113
Star Wars (film series) 7, 17, 46
Star Wars Force Trainer 159
Star Wars Galaxies 7, 139–40
Starcraft 81
stem cell research 59
Sundance Film Festival (2008) 143, 144
surface texturing 116

team games 100
television 58, 85, 114, 227
    Baer and 19
    console-based service 218–19
    family entertainment 20, 59
    and interaction 79, 136
    user expectations 136
    and virtual reality 160
    and younger children 64
'tetriminoes' 40
Tetris 40–42, 50, 122
text adventures 1–2
thatgamecompany 120
Thompson, Mark 226–7
Tolkien, J R R 45
Toy Story (film) 117
training 153, 157
    emergency medicine games 197–9
    military 188, 189, 190, 193
    see also education; learning
transnational relations 107–8

TripAdvisor 211
Triumph Studios 119
Trubshaw, Roy 45
Tunnel 228 show 133–4
Turbine Hall, Tate Modern, London 132
Twitter 89, 208, 212

Ultima Online 7, 100, 148
universities 225
University of Southern California 121, 186
Up (film) 117
US Center for Terrorism and Intelligence Studies (CETIS) 176
US Congress 182
US Department of Education 68
US Marine Combat Development Command 188
US Marines: First Recon unit 192
US military 187–8, 191, 194, 195
US Secret Service 68

value 151–2, 179–80
video arcades 87, 88
video game designer, as a career 37–8
video games
  addiction to 71–8
  and art 117–34
  big-budget 214, 222
  born in a technology institute 15–18

a business devoted to miracles 14–15
and children 58, 62, 63–5
compared with other games 6–7
complexity 9, 11, 39, 42, 50, 72, 73, 130, 171, 214
consumers 61–2
creation of 114–17
education 199–208
equality 103
and the family 89, 91
feedback 10
and films 137
first icons 20
games-based vs. real-life interactions 91–3
the hero's journey 46–7
and human behaviour 165–79
leadership in 98, 99, 101
as learning engines 6–7
as mainstream media activity 89
market for 22–3
military games 187–97
miniature games 126–9
mix of freedom and constraint in 102–3
moral panic 59
and music 135–6
nostalgia industry 52
perceived as played by adolescent males 87–8
players/non-players 59
power of 57–8, 223

progress by gaining experience 8

questions raised by 59–60

raising awareness 181–7

rapidly evolving 59

reviews 75

rules 5–7, 11

safety 58

as a social outlet 78–81

start of their commercial life 20

suitability for the digital age 28

teenage players (US) 90

time spent playing 29

two-player 88

and violence 60–61

and virtual theft 60–61

'visceral' thrills 10

Villiers, Justin 112–13, 114

violence in games

a minority interest 37, 82–3

regulation of 62, 224

and violence in life 65–71, 223

virtual currency 145–9

virtual economies 167, 169

virtual environments 142, 154, 172, 175

virtual epidemic 174–6

'virtual life' simulations 83

virtual reality 14, 138

goggles 141

and the Wii 160

virtual screens 14

virtual voting system 225

virtual worlds 33, 45–7, 59, 95, 103, 141, 146, 154, 155, 160, 166, 168, 170–73, 210, 211, 223, 225, 226, 233

war games 188

watches 28

Watts, Peter 133

Wells, H G 45

Wii Play 83

WILL Interactive Inc. 196

wireless control 14

women players 61

word processing 155, 157

work

virtual work 139–45

work/play separation 5, 145

World of Warcraft (WoW) ix, 30, 93–102, 105, 147, 149, 174, 175, 176, 217

Wortley, David 153–4, 156, 157, 160, 161

Wright, Evan: Generation Kill 191–2

writing, origin of 57, 111, 228

Xbox 360 games console 14, 215

XEODesign 49

Yahoo! 164

Yee, Nick 138–42, 150

YouTube 34, 164, 165

Zelda adventure games 200

Zelda II: The Adventure of Link 76